PORTRAIT OF AN ICE CAP

By the same Author

★

THE LAND THAT GOD GAVE CAIN

★

Published by Hodder & Stoughton

GINO WATKINS

VINEYARDS OF FRANCE
(With K. Baynes)

HEATHER MARY
(A Novel)

Steering a course on the Ice Cap *(Frontispiece)*

PORTRAIT OF
AN ICE CAP

WITH HUMAN FIGURES

By

J. M. SCOTT

1953

CHATTO & WINDUS

LONDON

PUBLISHED BY
CHATTO & WINDUS
LONDON

★

CLARKE, IRWIN & CO LTD
TORONTO

PRINTED IN GREAT BRITAIN

ACKNOWLEDGMENTS

In compiling this book I have been much assisted by the Royal Geographical Society and the Scott Polar Research Institute. The wartime details are largely derived from an article in the *Polar Record* by J. M. M. Blyth and from the book *War Below Zero* by Colonel Bernt Balchen, Major Corey Ford and Major Oliver La Farge. Most of the photographs were taken by Spencer Chapman or Iliffe Cozens on the British Arctic Air Route Expedition. Those facing pages 64 and 81 were taken on Martin Lindsay's British Trans-Greenland Expedition. The section and plan of the Ice Cap Station on page 113 was supplied by the *Polar Record*.

But it is evident that the real value of the book depends upon the diaries—and I cannot adequately thank those who let me quote from these personal records. There is a variety of bonds besides those of family which link men together, but I am sure none is stronger than that forged on an Arctic expedition.

J. M. S.

CONTENTS

ILLUSTRATIONS

ILLUSTRATIONS

DRAWINGS

CHAPTER I

The Canvas

WITHIN 2,000 miles of London and New York the Ice Age still exists. The biggest island in the world is almost entirely covered by permanent ice. This Ice Cap has been calculated to be 730,000 square miles in extent, about the area of England, Scotland, Wales, France, Italy, Holland, Belgium and Norway put together.

For millions of years the snow which has fallen in the central part of Greenland has not melted at the rate it fell. It has piled up and up, being constricted like flour dropped into a soup plate by the coastal rim of mountains. By its own weight all but the upper layers of snow has been pressed into solid ice.

In the middle line this ice is probably 6,000 or 7,000 feet thick. Resting on the foundation rocks it makes an undulating plateau with domes as high as 10,000 feet above sea-level, but falling—as our piled flour would fall—towards the edge. Here, by the outward push of the mass, the solid water is made to flow between the mountain gaps. The ends of these glaciers break off and fall into the sea, forming icebergs. So the Ice Cap excretes, balancing its meals of snow. That is one reason why it does not increase in size.

It sweats little, although at the lower levels in the summer-time the temperature may rise above freezing point. A far more important cause of loss must be the storms. Winds rising to well over a hundred miles an hour rush down from the high middle region to the sea, sweeping the snow before them in a stream so thick and deep that, crouching on the ice, one seems to be at the bottom of a turbid river.

So our first rough sketch of the Ice Cap shows a pear-shaped pile of ice and snow almost continental in extent, fringed by steep black mountains whose valleys are filled by glaciers, solid-frozen rivers.

Greenland's north coast is four hundred miles from the Pole. Its southern tip rests on the sixtieth parallel, the latitude of the Shetland Islands. But although it is comparatively close to the well-populated lands of the Northern Hemisphere it is completely different from them—and indifferent to them. It supports no life. There is nothing to eat on it: water everywhere but not a drop to drink. There are not even microbes in the air. Now and then a migratory bird comes down upon the Ice Cap and dies, as they must sometimes do in mid-ocean or in a desert. But the Ice Cap does not destroy the body. It preserves it, buries it, accepts it into its own cold immortality. It destroys nothing except life.

The human aborigines of Greenland are the Eskimos, or Greenlanders. They live in settlements of a few families each, scattered along the coast, and get their living from the sea. They never go onto the Ice Cap if they can help it. It is—or used to be in pre-Christian times—inhabited by evil spirits. In any case there are no seals there. The Eskimos are an essentially practical and unexacting people, ambitious only to keep their bellies full and to have a good party every now and then. Therefore they have survived.

The Norsemen made a colony in South Greenland about the year A.D. 1000. During four centuries—as long as from Elizabethan times to the present day—they tried to farm the narrow coastal strip. At one time there were 3,000 Christians living and working in Österbygd and Yesterbygd. They built stone houses and churches. They had sheep and cattle. But they all died, leaving only ruins and bones. As far as is known, they never ventured on the Ice Cap.

Nobody made a serious attempt to explore the Ice Cap until about eighty years ago. But it is with these pioneers that this book properly starts, for they, moving across the huge canvas, began to sketch the outlines of the picture.

Nansen made the first crossing of the Ice Cap from coast to coast in 1888, after Nordenskiold had penetrated it. Peary, de Quervain, Koch, Rasmussen followed, and there were several cuttings-off of segments. On such journeys the explorers had to be entirely self-contained, dragging with them everything that life requires—food, clothing, heating, shelter. Naturally these journeys were made as far as possible in the most favourable season, so no one knew what the middle of the Ice Cap was like in the middle of the winter.

To find this out two expeditions went to Greenland in 1930. One was of German scientists and was led by a professor in his fiftieth year. The other was led by an English undergraduate and consisted of fourteen men whose average age was twenty-five years. Both leaders intended, as a main part of their programme, to establish a Station on or near the high middle line of the Ice Cap, and to man it throughout a year. Both, in the main, achieved their object. One expedition suffered tragedy. The other, after sufficient hardship and anxiety, had a happy ending.

This book is concerned almost exclusively with one of these parties—the British Arctic Air Route Expedition led by Gino Watkins. In my object of painting a picture of an ice-age country with modern human beings living on it, I have a double advantage here. I have been allowed to use the diaries which different people wrote at the time, while in actual contact with the Ice Cap. And I was myself a member of the party. So I can give explanations where these are necessary.

These diary extracts form the most important part of the book, so I must expand on them. I promise that they are genuine and unadorned. Except for a few minor corrections of errors such as spelling and punctuation—natural enough in the circumstances— they are exactly as they were written in pencil and by candle-light in the tent, with cold fingers, waiting for the supper to cook or the socks to dry, and aching for sleep. They were not written for publication. They are unaffected expressions of the moment, without much of conventional style, sometimes in wrong syntax, scribbled records of thoughts and feelings and the day's events. Therefore they seem the best medium both for painting the portrait and sketching in the artists themselves as a foreground.

I have taken only two liberties. I have camouflaged some proprietary names, and I have altered certain adjectives and nouns. This latter change is made for accuracy of effect. Men without women use coarse words as a safety-valve until they become a meaningless habit. There is nothing to be ashamed of in this, but to the arm-chair reader it would give a false emphasis. Therefore in these instances I have substituted a conventional word, in italics to confess the liberty. Where immediate explanations have seemed necessary I have given these in square brackets.

It is interesting to speculate why, writing under such difficulties, people should have kept more than an essential record of events, for which a few words would have sufficed. I believe these diaries were a reaction to the natural desire for confidence, for expression to one person—the writer himself or somebody he loved. In fact they were a search for privacy.

The Ice Cap is lonely. But it is a truism that loneliness has little to do with privacy. We had there far fewer opportunities for privacy than in ordinary life. We slept, woke, dressed, cooked, ate, travelled together. Our natural functions were discharged within inches of each other. We were almost bestially public. Our only hope of privacy was in dreams or thoughts or, in a different form, by writing in our diaries. They were essentially private things. Only the lapse of time and the growing bonds of friendship have made it possible for me at last to publish extracts from them.

PORTRAIT OF AN ICE CAP

One diary was written both in loneliness and privacy. Augustine Courtauld gives the day by day account of the five months he spent alone, one hundred and forty miles away not only from the nearest man but from the nearest particle of life. I asked leave to use this personal record, then I asked the other members of the party for their diaries. Diffidently, but otherwise willingly, they let me have them.

The book is not scientific or historical. Nor is it intended as a travel book in the ordinary sense. It is a study of young men of an ordinary standard of education, tradition and imagination against the background of the Ice Cap. It is, I think, interesting to examine how much or how little one's standards and interests are affected by living the dog's life of an ice-age existence as rough as that which our prehistoric ancestors survived.

The Ice Cap from above the Base
Icebergs

Start of first journey : Ferrying dogs to the glacier-foot
Bingham, Riley, Lindsay, Rymill, Scott

CHAPTER II

First Impressions

OUR first sight of the Ice Cap was on a crystal-bright and windless morning in the summer of 1930 when the *Quest* steamed slowly into the glass-smooth water of a sheltered bay south of Angmagssalik. Although it was full daylight it was early, five or six o'clock. We came on deck and looked eagerly at the white Ice Cap and the dark mountains which held it back.

This was the landfall we had been aiming for, butting first through North Atlantic storms and then through pack-ice in an overloaded, overcrowded ship. This was the scene in which for a full year we would be most active actors, travelling great distances by dog sledge, on foot, in the open two-seater aeroplanes and in small boats. Each of the fourteen of us was prepared in the privacy of his imagination for a personal test, a tussle, for hardship and dangerous adventure. And we found this.

The scene was like a picture, it was so still. The *Quest* was the only moving thing—she and the silent V-shaped ripple of her wake. In the still fjord, sheltered from the ocean by a promontory, the icebergs lay as peacefully as water-lilies in a pond. But it was a pond with giants looking into it—the white Ice Cap thrusting forward and the black mountains standing erect to hold it back.

PORTRAIT OF AN ICE CAP

The Ice Cap reached out two arms towards the sea. The arm on the left—to the southward—fell steeply to the bay, here and there in sheer cliffs. It was comparable to a frozen waterfall or rapids. It was dramatic and forbidding. It was from here that now and then a piece of ice as large as a house broke off with a noise like thunder and fell with a tremendous splash, sending waves racing to rock the ship and all the floating bergs. That, in the perfect weather of our arrival, was the only loud sound or violent movement.

The other arm was less impressive. It stretched between a valley of bare rocks towards the sea but did not quite reach it. It was this right-hand glacier which offered the likelier road to the heart of the Ice Cap— the white desert behind. From water level we could see little of this white desert, for the first steep slopes hid the rest.

The mountains which held back the Ice Cap were imposing in their barren nakedness. To be exact there were plants, quite a variety of them, in the little sheltered valleys or clustering round the tarns of this narrow coastal strip. But we could not see them from the ship. We could see only ice and rock, water and sky.

This may sound bleak. It was anything but that. Certainly the Ice Cap met the sky in a cold white line against the blue. But nearer at hand where the ice was broken, and particularly where it was floating in the transparent water, it was as full of colours as jewels are—emerald, aquamarine, turquoise and mother-of-pearl. We had never guessed there could be so many nuances of greens and blues and violets. These subtle shades were set off to best advantage against the dominant white and black. And the whole world was so calm and bright. It was fairyland.

But we had work to do. We worked with tremendous energy, in night and day shifts, sometimes both, excited by the novelty of everything, helped by the perfect weather. The ship was unloaded, the hut built, the wireless masts erected, the reconnaissances made. . . . We had sailed into the bay on July 26th. Within a fortnight we were ready for the first journeys.

There were fourteen of us. The leader was Gino Watkins. He was then twenty-three, two years younger than the average of the party. He had led two previous expeditions to the North. One of them had been to Labrador, where I had travelled with him. Augustine Courtauld had also been to the Arctic before, although only on summer expeditions. Spencer Chapman had been to Iceland, studying birds. John Rymill came from Australia. Hampton, Riley, Stephenson and Wager had recently taken their degrees at Cambridge. The rest were from the Services—Bingham from the Navy, Lemon and Lindsay from the Army, D'Aeth and Cozens from the R.A.F.

Most of the party were to start work by sailing north along the coast, to map it from small boats and by aerial photography. Lemon was to stay at the Base and keep in touch with them by wireless. The remaining five—Martin Lindsay, Quintin Riley, Doc Bingham, John Rymill and I—were going to sledge in onto the Ice Cap and set up the Central Weather Station.

Martin and Quintin would take the first turn at manning the Station.

This journey gave us our first experience of the Ice Cap. It deceived us. The work was hard enough, the surface rough enough, and the weather just cold enough when we had travelled some distance and climbed to five or six thousand feet, to make us think that we were meeting and overcoming the hardships and difficulties of the Ice Age. I suppose we were, but the Ice Age must have been quite pleasant in summer —at any rate if one did not have to travel far. It was warm. We were deceived because it was impossible to imagine how completely different conditions would be in three months' time, or with what drastic sudden-ness the change would come.

.   .   .   .   .

The others helped us to carry the loads and lead the dogs up the rocks to the foot of the glacier. There they said good-bye and returned to the ship to prepare for their own boat and aeroplane journeys.

They left us standing among a pile of boxes, bags and furled tents, a snake pit of alpine ropes, lash lines and traces, and twenty-eight more or less strange huskies—four sledge teams. I was the only one who had driven dogs before. John Rymill was a skier but the other three had no more than the ordinary citizen's experience of snow. In front of us the glacier stretched up and up like an ancient giant's stairway to the Ice Cap proper. But it was rougher than the roughest stairway. The surface was bare ice since all the snow had melted—hard, and sharp in places, yet very slippery. The loads had to be sorted and distributed between the sledges. Nansen sledges are pliant. Their efficiency depends upon their being able to move like lizards over inequalities, turning easily, bending and undulating. To achieve this the load must be balanced with its centre of gravity just so, and it must be lashed to the sledge just so, firmly enough to resist violent movement.

The dogs had to be harnessed—by strange masters who did not know the strict conventions of each team. Worst of all, they had to have boots—little canvas bags —tied over their pads to protect them from the sharp needles of bare ice. They objected to this. . . . We had risen from our beds at six o'clock and it was almost noon before we at last got under way—with a great deal of heaving and shouting, a scrabbling of padded paws, and the creak and slither of sledges climbing and skidding among hummocks of ice.

But the diary entries for that night do not suggest that anybody felt overawed. Bingham wrote: "Packed sledges and started our journey. Made about two and a half miles all day over very rough country, and camped the night at the base of the steep ice cliff where caught by rain before getting into camp."

This steep slope at the head of the glacier, almost an ice fall, was afterward referred to in print—politely— as Bugbear Bank. On this occasion it took us two days to get up it, all of us working together with a half-load at a time, shoving at the sledge or hauling on all fours beside the dogs.

But the weather was warm and when we were thirsty we could find water to drink: when we had a chance to rest we could relax—neither of which pleasures can be enjoyed when it is cold. Above Bugbear there was snow on the ice, but it was wet and stained with puddles. Exhausting though the work might be, the Ice Cap had not yet used either of its two main weapons—cold and wind.

But it used others. The ice was still comparatively shallow. In its slow movement it was affected by the unequal surface of the rock floor. It had cracked into crevasses, many of them hidden by a thin layer of snow. There were two separate mazes of crevasses, and it took us another three days to find a way through them, marking the route with red flags. All this time the coastal mountains were to one side or close behind us.

Beyond the crevasses we set up an extra large red flag on a nine-foot bamboo. (It was afterwards called the Big Flag Depot.) From here we could travel straight and comparatively fast upon our course. Going on, but looking back over our shoulders every now and then, we saw the mountains dropping gradually below the horizon. First one and then another sank out of sight. Within a day there was nothing to be seen except snow and our own small party. The sky came down to the circular white horizon. We had lost the land by the convex slope of the Ice Cap as at sea one loses it by the curvature of the earth.

I am describing the journey very briefly. It was only a summer journey, scarcely more testing than any arduous holiday. Close interest comes with winter, the true season of the North. But it will be best to make a few points now for the better understanding of later journeys.

The position of the Ice Cap Station had been calculated as the point where the intended air route would cross the spine of the Ice Cap. From the Big Flag inland of the crevasses we navigated towards this point much as one navigates at sea, steering a calculated compass course and checking it by astronomical observations. John Rymill was navigator, using a theodolite and time-signal set to find our longitude and latitude. Martin Lindsay was his assistant. Quintin Riley was the meteorologist. Bingham was the doctor and, being a sailor, a most handy man. I was the dog master and general instructor. But already my mystery had dissolved into common knowledge. Dog driving on the featureless Ice Cap only meant slogging on in single file. The driver's task was no more than starting his sledge, cursing the dogs into action and untangling their traces every now and then, and—most exacting—preventing the heavily laden sledge from upsetting on the waves of wind-blown snow.

We marked the route at half-mile intervals with small red bunting flags fixed to three-foot bamboos. We measured the distances by means of a cyclometer wheel towed behind the leading sledge. We were at great pains to place these flags exactly in line and on the proper course. And we took care to plant them securely, hammering them into the almost chalk-hard *névé* and patting down a little tower about the base.

I calculated that we spent at least six minutes erecting each. We kept on travelling as long as it was clear or light enough to see one flag from another. Each twenty-four hours was divided roughly as follows: Breakfasting, breaking camp and loading sledges—4½ hours. Morning travel—4 hours. Lunch—½ hour. Afternoon travel—4½ hours. Pitching tents, feeding dogs and ourselves—3 hours. Reading, writing, mending and drying socks and gloves—1 hour. Sleep—6½ hours. This routine was only interrupted by halts for observations, or by bad weather.

Thus, until August 28th, we travelled towards the chosen point over the white featureless plateau. We were climbing all the time—up to about 9,000 feet above sea-level. The surface was not smooth. It was something like a rippled ocean swell, the ripples being wind drifts and the swell long undulations or dunes as much as half a mile from crest to crest.

When we reached the chosen point we unloaded from our sledges the special tent, the numerous instruments, five sledging boxes—two men's full rations for five weeks (but being static they would not need full rations); a bag of beans; peas and prunes, some tea, and twenty-four gallons of paraffin. Riley and Lindsay were to live here on these supplies until the first relief came up from the Base one hundred and forty miles away along the line of little red flags which marked the way.

CHAPTER III

Riley and Lindsay
at the Ice Cap Station

O N August 28th Quintin Riley wrote in his diary:
"Well, here we are—Martin and I—for six or
eight weeks. A lovely view, just nothing stretching in
front of us."

John Rymill, Doc Bingham and I remained for a
day and a half longer to help them set up the tent.
This was a thing which in shape was like an opened
umbrella without the handle. It had eight curved
wooden ribs and a double-canvas cover. It was nine feet
in diameter and gave a headroom under the apex of
just over six feet. Passing through the apex—as the
end of an umbrella projects from the top—was a short
length of brass tubing to act as a ventilator. There was
no door or window. Entrance was by means of a
twenty-foot-long burrow which came up in the floor.
Theoretically, this was the best type of entrance, for
since cold air is heavier than hot, it would only rise
from the burrow into the tent as it was required, when
one opened the valve of the ventilator. Having put up
the tent and dug the burrow we held an inaugural
dinner—although only of sledging rations—in what
was thereafter called the Ice Cap Station.

Next morning—I quote Riley again—"All had
breakfast together, after which preparations were

made for the departure of Jamie, Rymill and Bingham. The party left lickerty split about 4 p.m. It was getting cold so Martin and I went back and had a cup of cocoa. We tidied up a bit outside and settled our things inside. After supper Martin and I played chess in which he thought of a very pretty mate. A chapter of *Vanity Fair* and so to bed."

My own diary for the evening reads: "Put nine dogs onto each sledge and went off at a grand pace. 20·6 miles in 4½ hours."

Martin and Quintin were already that distance from any sort of company. They were there to make meteorological observations every three hours, but here I am more concerned with how they got on together and how they lived.

They were different in background and interests. Martin described himself—not very accurately—as a typical soldier. He had been in India and Africa, had done some big game shooting, and at home enjoyed hunting and the country-house week-end. In personal habits he tended to be casual and to lose things. Quintin had been at Cambridge, where he had coxed his boat. Now the only sport he talked about was yachting. His other main topics, as well as I can remember them, were religion and his family. He was an ardent and dogmatic churchman, and very much wrapped up in his home in Jersey where his father, Athelstan Riley, lived in the Manoir de la Trinité. In personal habits he tended to be fussy and precise. More than most of us he was interested in his comfort. He had brought a rubber hot-water bottle with him on the Ice Cap. Economising in fuel, we had had on the way up to make porridge out of the same water next morning.

In his diary, Quintin wrote on August 31st: "I feel Martin will be most admirable. Nothing upsets him and he is one of the most good-natured people I have ever met. In fact an excellent person for this sort of game."

Martin Lindsay wrote later (his diary has been destroyed, but I quote from *Those Greenland Days*): "We always behaved quite naturally, and no effort had to be made to give and take. This is all the more odd, as in both temperament and tastes we had practically nothing in common. And although the days we spent together on the Ice Cap broke down all barriers so that we learned just everything about each other, we have, strange to say, never returned to the same intimacy."

Looking back, it was not strange at all. However different their temperaments might otherwise be, they were both men of the type which volunteers. (This was brought out once again in the war.) They shared a taste for what they were doing. They shared a point of view in those primitive conditions as two men never could in the crowded, varied life at home—however much they had in common. If they returned now to the Ice Cap they would again share, single-mindedly, the same interest, talking as an amusing recreation of themselves at home as of other people in another life.

Their interest apart from the duty of weather study was to make a comfortable home. Examples of this house-pride instinct are frequent in the diaries, as you will see. For instance, Quintin and Martin "tidied up a bit" as soon as they were left alone. Each occupant of the Ice Cap Station was anxious to make and keep the place as neat as possible so that it would be appreciated by the relieving party. Yet the first thing each relief recorded when he was left alone was: "Tidied up the mess."

Martin and Quintin had ample scope for improvements, for we had only helped them to erect the tent. Their first task was to set up the instruments—the nephoscope, the Stevenson screen and its contents, and what Martin called the whirligig for measuring the speed of the wind. But they found time for satisfying their morale and comfort.

"*August* 31*st*—I hung my crucifix over my sleeping-bag and we hoisted the Union Jack outside, and so we have both Christian and National emblems erected.

"*September* 2*nd*—Martin dug a capital *ice closet*. A deep pit, and snow from it will give excellent shelter. He has placed a sledge over the pit so as to make a seat. This should be most comfortable.

"*September* 4*th*—We had difficulty getting out as our tunnel was choked by yesterday's snow. We spent all the morning clearing away drifts. The *i.c.* has been filled up too. Very annoying. . . .

"*September* 11*th*—Temp. last night down to minus 14 degrees F. A lot of hoar-frost in the tent this morning. A lovely day, blue sky and sun. . . . Sat outside and read a book. . . . In p.m. started to build a snow house over the *i.c.*

"*September* 14*th, Sunday*—We rested from our house building this day. Morn and p.m. I spent much time sitting in the yard reading, temp. minus 1 degree F. to 6 degrees F., but nice and warm in the sun. I read a chapter of St. Paul's Epistle to the Romans and St. John's Gospel, also two or three chapters of the *Imitation of Christ*. As I have left my St. Swithun's [a devotional book] behind this is the most I can do. Temp. minus 23·8 degrees F.

"*September* 16*th*—Snowed all day but not heavily. . . . I designed the accommodation plan for my Brixham trawler till fifteen hours and then went and dug for an hour. M. began his story for *Blackwood's Magazine*.

"Temp. reached 16 degrees today. It feels quite warm. M. even complained it was too warm tonight in the house. It is curious how changed one is over the cold. When we first met 16 degrees of frost on the way up we thought it awful. Now we find it comparatively hot, but it has been nice not to find hoar-frost from one's breath on one's pillow in the morning. A game of chess I won.

"*September* 17*th*—Finished *Wuthering Heights*, a delightful book. M. a headache—lack of exercise? Wash tonight.

"*September* 18*th*—A sunny day. Both dug in a.m. and p.m. . . . We expect Rymill and Lemon with the wireless any day now.

"*September* 19*th*—We have decided to build a snow house in case our successors have to move, finding the tent too cold. We are building it alongside the tent, and the one tunnel will do for both. We shall also keep piling snow on this tent to try to keep it warm.

"*September 28th*—We continued building snow house in the morning. In the afternoon we read and later discussed plans for abandoning should nobody turn up during the next fortnight. We could stay here about another three weeks and then have ten days' food to get us back to the Base on small rations, but I trust this will not be necessary."

Martin Lindsay enlarged upon this talk of walking out: "There was not time at the beginning of the expedition to get up to the Station all the food required for the year; and although this was desirable it did not appear in any way essential. So the plan was that every relief party sledging up there would take their own supplies with them. The safety margin lay in the understanding that if at any time a long-overdue relief did not arrive, then the garrison would haul down the flag and walk out without dishonour.

"So, like subsequent occupants of the Station, Quintin and I spent long hours discussing the imaginary breakdown of the party that was on the way up to us, and what we should do when we were reduced to the sweepings and scraping of the last ration box. . . . Neither of us intended to be a martyr to meteorology. So we made all our plans for walking out when we were reduced to just a little less than the bare minimum for the homeward journey. We never had the slightest doubt that we would be relieved in due course; but it is always fun to make a desperate resolve which you know perfectly well you will not have the bother of carrying out."

For other recreation they played chess every night,

read aloud from the *Oxford Book of English Verse*, and read to themselves from the small library which was increased with the arrival of each relief.

They had their stock jokes. When the snow slipped down the canvas dome of the tent, it was: "That cat's on the roof again." At breakfast: "The postman's late," and "Is there anything in the paper, dear?" They spent many hours in the evening, as a sort of game, trying to light the patent lamp, which apparently objected to the low atmospheric pressure at 9,000 feet, or to the fugginess of the tent. Also Riley tried a number of cooking experiments. But with only peas and prunes and sledging rations as ingredients, he admitted sadly that these were not really worth the trouble.

They had less spare time, however, than all this suggests. Every three hours between seven in the morning and ten at night one of them had to dress up (if he were not working outside already), crawl up through the burrow, make a tour of the instruments, and then crawl down again to shake and dust the snow off his clothes.

Lindsay wrote that the 7 a.m. observation was the worst. "On the other hand, seven of an evening at this time of year is an hour enchanted. With the setting sun the western sky floods slowly into the most extraordinary extremes of colour—brilliant contrasts of pink, pale blue and orange, purple and gold. It is not like the brief sunset of the tropics, where the glow dies out in a second, all the colours become ashen and night seems to prepare and arrive in a moment. Instead the sun lingers on well into the twilight as if it were reluctant to go and take away one of the few consolations of this barren land; and long afterwards there remains a pink flush on the distant horizon, which is reflected on the sky by the clouds. The stillness is unbroken save by the flapping of the flag as the wind comes and goes, and sometimes the sighing of the snow as it speeds along the ground. Ten o'clock has its delights, too, in the beauty of the northern lights, a muster of dim lances, close serried, standing erect in the sky."

Besides the observations, there was the housework —cooking, mending and a little washing—the digging away of drifted snow, and the construction of the second snow house, which was intended as alternative living quarters—and something rather special in the way of design.

"*September 22nd* [Riley]—We finished the second tier of the snow house although we had difficulty with the architecture over the cupboard. I struck a bad vein of snow and cut out five bricks which all broke. . . .

"*September 23rd*—A bad day as far as the snow house went. Blocks wouldn't cut well and we couldn't get the third tier started. . . . No signs of Lemon and Rymill. A most wonderful aurora tonight, the sky was practically covered with it.

"*September 24th*—We managed to overcome the difficulties with the snow house and finished the third tier. Of course Martin's cupboard is the real cause of difficulty. I don't think Stefansson or Eskimos build snow houses with cupboards. However we do, and it now seems satisfactory.

Riley at the Ice Cap Station—note
the entrance to the tunnel

Twenty miles in ... losing the coastal mountains

"*September 26th*—It is surprising how little we eat now. One plate of porridge for breakfast, half a biscuit and butter and a little chocolate for lunch, and half a biscuit and butter for tea. A few peas and a plate of pemmican, very thin though, for dinner, with prunes on alternate nights and cod-liver oil of course, and on this we feel very well fed. . . . Two games of chess tonight both of which I won. M. lost his queen in both of them. He doesn't seem much use without her.

"*September 29th*—It snowed most of the day, keeping us indoors. I am reading *Jane Eyre* which I find hard to put down.

"*October 1st, Wednesday*—We cleared up the yard most of the day. . . . No sign of travellers. . . .

"*October 2nd, Thursday*—Snow all a.m. I mended some shoes. Just going out for a breather about 3.30 —still snowing—when I heard *Uhe, Uhe* and a bark. Yes, Jamie, Gino, Rymill, Freddy, Bingham and D'Aeth all arriving. Had a grand dinner. Gino and Jamie slept in our snow house. Both houses have met with Gino's approval I am glad to say."

CHAPTER IV

Winter Comes Suddenly

THESE reunions at the Ice Cap Station made up for all the weariness, cold, boredom and aggravating struggle of a journey. There was very little to enjoy while we were travelling. We lived in the future. "If we can keep up such an average we shall arrive in x days." The same phrase, with modifications due to better or worse weather and snow conditions, went round and round in our brains however hard we tried to escape from the parrot-like repetition.

When we arrived there was an explosion of companionship, of talk and special cooking and more talk, of tobacco smoke and singing—concentrated life within a few square yards of the lifeless Ice Cap. It lasted a day or two, and then we separated on our various journeys, knowing nothing about what was happening to anybody else. Two miles away and you felt as much separated as if it were two hundred.

Lindsay and Riley were not being relieved by Rymill and Lemon with the wireless transmitting set as they had expected. They were not surprised. Gino's plans varied with the unknown conditions. The account which Rymill, Bingham and I had brought back of our comparatively easy journey had none-the-less given him a hint of what might follow. Radio communication could wait: food and fuel first. So the 'experienced' three of the first journey came back, each with a different half section. John Rymill was with Freddy Chapman, bringing in stores. Doc Bingham was with Jimmy D'Aeth, travelling up to relieve Quintin and Martin but carrying such effective stores as they could. (Effective stores were what could be left at the destination as opposed to what was consumed on the journey out and back.) I was with Gino Watkins, who had come in to have a look at things before starting on our southern journey.

The whole expedition had not been together since the *Quest* sailed into the Base Fjord, and they were not to be together until the next summer. But here was half the party crowded into the Ice Cap Station tent. Besides gossip and eating and smoking and singing there was a chance for talking plans.

Gino said that Chapman, who had now done a hundred and forty miles of dog sledging, should lead another journey up to the Ice Cap Station as soon as possible after his return to the Base. There were plenty of people now at the Base, the other half of the expedition—seven in all. Hampton and Stephenson were to be the next relief of the Station. Lemon was to come up to install the transmitting set and show them how to use it, and then return. Besides these, as big a load-carrying party as possible was to sledge in stores.

With this decided, we parted after two nights and a day. Freddy Chapman and Rymill, Martin Lindsay and Quintin Riley set off for the coast. Watkins and I started on our southern journey, and Surgeon Lieutenant Bingham and Squadron Leader D'Aeth began their garrison at the Ice Cap Station.

I quote extracts from Doc Bingham's diary for the day after Chapman's party had left.

"*October 5th*—Got up fairly early and cooked breakfast for Watkins and Scott who were lashing up their sledges, etc. Saw them started on their journey and so were left alone. Started in right away to spring-clean the tent. It was a long job. We built two divans with ration boxes. . . . Put all our clothes and gear into the empty ones. Much warmer with the divans. Lots of work ahead. Hope to clean up the courtyard tomorrow. Cold but nice day. The observations are a nuisance, but why else would we be here?

"*October 6th*—Did observations at seven but retired to bed again. After breakfast tidied up all the courtyard and put stores into snow house. Then started in to cut snow blocks which at first gave us some trouble. After lunch started to build a snow house round the big tent. This is octagonal and I finished one side while D'Aeth worked at some means of making the *lamp* burn in the tent. This has not been managed before and would mean greatly added comfort. . . . Got a four-gallon paraffin tin and cut off the top. Also cut a square trap-door at the bottom of one side. Inside this we set a sugar tin upside down with a round hole cut in its bottom and another in its side facing the trap-door in the large tin. Then made a funnel out of the cardboard casings round the lemon-juice bottles and tied this on to the trap-door in the large tin, leading the other end down the tunnel. Put lamp on sugar tin and lit it. This was successful from four till seven, but cooking was too much for it so we reverted to a candle. . . .

"*October 8th*—Lay up all day in the tent as it was blowing a gale and snowing. Atmosphere in tent much better and *lamp* going well. Temperature rose to zero. Started a letter to mother which will probably be a long one and may not get to her for nearly a year. Longing thoughts of the mail which should be at the Base for me by now.

"*October 11th*—Cold. Dug out the tunnel of the tent and made it much longer while D'Aeth cut blocks to roof the passage part. After lunch we roofed over the passage so that our tunnel is much longer and the roofed part deep enough to stand upright in.

"*October 14th*—Continued digging out the courtyard and building the wall. D'Aeth cutting snow blocks for new snow house. Lamp worked well and we had a most comfortable evening reading.

"*October 17th*—Evenings very comfortable now and a pleasure to look forward to.

"*October 18th*—Finished the snow house this morning. After lunch started to dig the essential parts of the courtyard again so as to have it neat and tidy for Sunday. . . .

"*October 19th, Sunday*—Intended having a nice restful day but after breakfast started in to clean our cooking pots which were in a filthy mess. After that went on to scrape the ice and hoar-frost off the bottom of the tent. . . . The tent feels much more comfortable and clean since the deer skins were shaken out.

"*October 22nd*—Continued to dig out courtyard and build up wall. . . . Place is now as I would like it to be when relieving party arrives.

"*October 26th, Sunday*— . . . Had a grand wash and clipped the beard. Also change of clothes. Expect to see the relieving party here in about ten days from now. Wrote another addition to mother's letter. Being Sunday we had a day of rest. Watkins and Scott left us three weeks today so they should be turning north about now."

    .   .   .   .   .

On the Ice Cap there are only two seasons—summer and winter. There is no vegetation to fade and shed its leaves, or sprout and flower. Therefore neither autumn nor spring is recognisable. There is only a mild season and a cold season.

Cold causes various inconveniences. It paints the tent with hoar-frost directly the stove is extinguished. Often you wake up with your hair frozen to the canvas, and your fingers stick to the cooking pots when you first touch them in the morning. Outside everything takes longer to do because your brain and muscles work more slowly. When travelling you become painfully thirsty because the air is so dry, and when you camp the rapidly freezing sweat makes your clothes go stiff as tin. Cold makes the sledge drag heavily. Sledge runners, skis and skates slide magically only because by their pressure they thaw out a lubricating film of moisture. That happens at ordinary temperatures. But when it is really cold, ice is like rock and snow as dry as sand.

WINTER COMES SUDDENLY

Yet it is not cold alone that makes the winter. It is wind—wind which multiplies the effects of cold quite ten times over. The wind may come after the first cold. It may come suddenly and without warning. When it does, there is no longer any doubt that it is winter on the Ice Cap.

Gino and I had started from the I.C.S. while it was still summer, although the tail end of it. At first the thermometer rarely dropped below minus 20 degrees F., which is the temperature at which cold begins to be a practical obstacle, not merely a discomfort. After the first week we got some minus thirties and forties, but there was no wind. We had started with fully loaded sledges which gave us a range of three weeks out and three weeks back. We were going to travel as far as we could southward down the spine of the Ice Cap to chart its contour, then to turn straight for the Base, thus completing a triangular course.

It was a journey that we had talked about a lot. We saw no reason why we should not average fifteen miles a day—do about three hundred miles during the three weeks out. After all, we were supposed to be the experts. . . . I have said there was little or no present pleasure in a journey. But there was a tremendous satisfaction in achieving big distances, in putting up a record.

As it turned out we put up no record, unless it was for slowness. It was the most extraordinary experience. The Ice Cap was virtually flat and there were no big drifts. The snow was rarely cold enough to be sandy. The weather was quite favourable. The dogs appeared to be in good physical condition and were getting their full ration. We ourselves were perfectly fit and urgently anxious to go fast. Yet in the first half of the journey we averaged less than five miles a day. We covered only ninety miles.

Puzzled and exasperated we blamed the dogs. We had petted and encouraged them. We had cursed and beaten them. We had gone in front to break the trail and give them something to look at. We had given them extra food from our own ration boxes. We had tried everything we knew. There was nothing wrong with them physically, and the loads were getting lighter by about twenty pounds a day. But they remained listless. At the slightest check they sat down and it was the very devil to get them moving again.

As soon as we turned for home the dogs woke up. In three days we did thirty miles, a third of the distance we had covered in the three weeks out. One could not actually complain about a good speed, but it was maddening that dogs with so much life in them should have made fools of us. . . .

That night, soon after we had blown the candle out, something like a breaking wave struck against the tent. There was a moment of silence while we lay in our sleeping-bags and listened, and then it struck again. Soon the bamboo poles were creaking and the canvas was flapping like the sail of a tacking yacht. Next morning, poking our heads out, we saw the drift flowing by 100 feet deep. Our tent was the only obstacle in the path of the semi-solid wind. It was battered continually and a great bank formed behind it. "The wretched dogs," says my diary, "could get no shelter, for the holes we had dug for them had drifted up. They looked very unhappy with their tails between their legs and their eyes full of snow."

And yet it was the dogs, in their inexplicable way, which had given us a chance. The weather, as we were soon to discover, had broken completely. Winter had come. The storms, fantastic things, went on for days together. The intervals were difficult enough, with awkward drifts and crevasses as we crossed above the head of a big fjord. We were travelling along a low contour of the Ice Cap, where the downhill winds reached about their maximum velocity. But the dogs were magnificent and made the most of every travelling day.

While we lay up in the battered tent during the storms there were two things which we principally discussed. The first was the behaviour of the dogs. We were confident that we would get back to the Base—although with little to spare. But it would have been a different story if the dogs had not suddenly risen to the occasion. On the other hand, if they had gone well from the start—dogs generally go better at the start—and had taken us two or three hundred miles south, we did not see how we could have got back.

The other subject of discussion was Chapman's relief journey. We had been able to cut our own journey and run for it. But he could not do that, whatever the weather, because he had got to reach the Ice Cap Station and relieve Bingham and D'Aeth, who would have finished most of their supplies. It was now the beginning of November. We had parted at the Ice Cap Station on October 4th. With light sledges he should have done a rapid journey to the Base—say a week or ten days. If he had managed to make a quick turn round he might, we thought, have got off again about October 20th—over a fortnight ago. In that case he should, before the weather broke, have passed through the coastal zone where we were and where the storms were no doubt strongest. In optimistic moments Gino and I pictured him (as Bingham and D'Aeth were picturing him) at or near the Ice Cap Station. We expected that he might return to the Base soon after we got there ourselves.

On November 10th Gino picked up from the snow a piece of red cotton thread. That meant that we were converging on the line of flags which marked the route from the Base to the I.C.S.

Shortly after this we saw a cluster of black dots away in front of us. It is very difficult on the featureless Ice Cap to judge distances and therefore the size of what you see. But soon we knew that they were men and dogs. Chapman's party! Our first reaction was of joy, for they must be coming out having relieved and restocked the Station in record time.

But as we hurried towards them, they pausing to wait for us, we thought with fear of another explanation—that they were only just beginning their journey.

CHAPTER V

Fifteen Miles in Fifteen Days

CHAPMAN had made one previous journey to the Ice Cap Station and back. The rest of the party of six had never driven dogs before. Nobody can have had a harder introduction to this form of travel.

I will recapitulate. Gino had given instructions that Stephenson, the chief surveyor, and Hampton, the second pilot and mechanic, were to relieve Bingham and D'Aeth at the Station. Chapman was to take them in as soon as possible and with as large a party as could be spared. Of these Lieutenant Lemon, the sapper and wireless operator, should be one, for it was intended to establish radio communication between the I.C.S. and the Base in case it should be possible to fly in stores during the winter. The rest of the organisation was left to the leader. His responsibility was considerable—to relieve Bingham and D'Aeth and deliver enough stores to the Station to enable the new couple to maintain it until they could be relieved the next year.

That was typical of Gino's orders. He fully explained intentions and left the details to the man concerned. Also he seemed to think that most people were capable of more than they themselves had previously believed. The Ice Cap was a new field.

Nobody could have led this difficult journey better

than Chapman did. He had faith and vision. He was a tremendous driver—chiefly of himself. He had reserves of imaginative recreation, and he was an unconquerable optimist.

Three of Chapman's party have already been mentioned—Lemon, Hampton and Stephenson—sapper, flying man and surveyor. The other two were Wager, the geologist and an experienced mountaineer, and Augustine Courtauld. Courtauld was a skilful surveyor, had twice previously visited the Arctic on summer expeditions, and was the only man of the party besides Watkins who was a member of the Committee. There would be a supporting party of three men, Rymill, Cozens and Lindsay.

The start was delayed by bad weather. Early in October the first Ice Cap storm rushed down upon the Base. The wind gauge registered 129 m.p.h.—and then blew away. Many other things blew away as well, and the stores were scattered far and wide. It was like a bombing raid made to disorganise an attack.

The journey which followed is described by means of extracts from the diaries of four of the men who took part in it.

October 25th, Saturday

WAGER — We were to have started for the Ice Cap Base about 5 a.m. when a wind sprang up, the same in character but not so strong as the gale of ten days ago. There was the same clear sky except for one or two almost still high clouds and the wind was again gusty, but it was well below freezing, probably averaging about 28 degrees to 30 degrees most of the day. Snow was blowing off the glacier in clouds, and a blizzard was clearly going on there. So we had a day of comparative peace at the Base.

October 26th, Sunday

WAGER — Wind dropped and a little snow falling. A great round up to catch the vixen of my team but she disappeared—presumably hiding. An hour later Freddie caught her. Freddie is in good form running every-thing. This trip is his responsibility. First load went over [the fjord to the foot of the glacier] about 9 a.m. Helped Freddie and Lemon off by the second boat at noon. Ice apparently allowed the boat to get to the peninsula south of the glacier.

Fed the dogs on seal meat on landing and took a load up. Already getting dark. Steve [Stephenson] and I had the torn tent and retired as soon as possible— about 6.30. Reindeer skin and bag soft and luxurious.

CHAPMAN — The supporting party — Rymill, Cozens and Lindsay—are in a single small alpine tent. I hope we shall have their help till the Big Flag. Over-cast tonight and warm: probably a blizzard tomorrow.

October 27th, Monday

COURTAULD — A wind got up when we were getting out of our tents at 4 a.m. It blew off the inland ice and was intensely cold. It rapidly increased to gale force and by the time we had carried up one load from the bottom it was blowing the snow off the glacier in clouds and endangering the tents.

WAGER — Into tent for lunch. Wind increasing.

Nothing done all afternoon. At 4 p.m. fed dogs. Pink on the distant hills and clear sky. The clouds of fine snow were behaving and looking exactly like Scotch mist. Freddie rationed out candles and lime juice, etc. More pemmican bags on tent [on the outer flaps of the tent to hold them down. Pegs are little use in ice or snow]. Wind increasing. Put food out of tins into bags [to save weight]. Supper of pemmican and pea-flour, and tea and biscuits. Wind now terrific in gusts.

Again with the sun out, and while in our tent for lunch, we saw the good effect of standing on emerald-coloured luminous ice.

October 28th, Tuesday

WAGER — Last night the wind increased to a gale. We barricaded the walls with kit-bags and luggage and kept these in position by ourselves lying down between them and being ourselves in contact, holding them out. We could not sleep. At about 11 p.m. Freddie and Lemon's tent blew down for the third time that day despite their having moved it to another place. It gave them warning so that they had got their boots on. Nevertheless the outer cover of the tent was carried away. Freddie into Courtauld's and Ham's [Hampton's] tent and Lemon into the small mountain tent which had already Rymill, Cozens and Martin in it. They took the poles out and held it down over them. The wind changed a little towards east and then blew in violent gusts with a complete calm between. At about 2 a.m. it stopped suddenly and we slept till 4 a.m.

CHAPMAN — The wind stopped all at once. It was as if the earth had suddenly stopped spinning, and we realised how tremendous the nervous strain had been.

WAGER — A few gusts as we got up, and it was decided to move the tents 200 yards on to the moraine. This took all morning. I went off to look for lost things and walked almost straight to the cover of Freddie's tent. Quintin, with Arapika and Gustari [an Eskimo boy and girl], arrived. Arapika was put on to sewing the tent covers.

Clouds were approaching from the sea and snow seemed imminent, but we lashed our sledge, put on crampons and dog shoes and began to take it up with six men. The going was better than expected and some of us came back for another load. The moral effect of getting two loads to Bugbear is considerable.

Beautiful study in blues, greys and whites as we came back, with our fjord spread out below in the dusk.

My dogs have not cut [bitten through] a single trace—the only team so well behaved.

October 29th, Wednesday

CHAPMAN — Up at 4.30. High starlit morning. Sirius shining very bright just over the snow-covered Base mountains, and Orion's belt well up in the sky. Heard the harsh regular bark of an Arctic fox down by the shore. As soon as it was light enough, four men took a load up to start work on Bugbear.

WAGER — A cold evening, and again pink snow for an hour at sunset, and then fine blues and greys as we came down the glacier. This is the only time we have to look round [when returning after taking up a half-load].

October 30th, Thursday

WAGER — Awoke about 2 a.m. and heard the wind roaring in the distance though there was not even a light breeze on the tents. These winds are remarkably local, as the Helm in Edenside. At 3.30 the wind reached us in gusts, and Steve got out and put more stones round the tent. Did not get up at four as wind was high. By six it had completely stopped. There was a little high cirrus pinked by the dawn sun, and the almost constant cloud bank out to sea. Rymill went up onto the glacier and reported considerable scattering of gear but apparently nothing lost.

After breakfast and taking down tents, began lashing the last two sledges. I went off to see if anything had collected in the cave under the side of the glacier where other things had been found, and there collected a two-gallon petrol tin and a kit-bag. Steve's dogs were good for five minutes and then wanted a rest. Lemon's dogs worked far better than anyone expected, even the one that bites.

By the time we reached Bugbear a blizzard was blowing.

STEPHENSON — The blizzard began in full, driving powdery snow into everything—pockets, boxes, and down our necks. It was bitterly cold and icicles formed on our eyelashes making us quite blind. Our wool helmets were frozen, with great lumps of ice on

Chapman

Courtauld

Stephenson

Wager

Bugbear Bank : Sledging up the lower slopes
Block and tackle on the upper slopes

our eyebrows and chins. We then had to pitch the tent, the very devil of a job. A brief interval while I cut Wager's beard, he having found it too long for the ice. However we got the tent up and the kit inside. I then had to cut up some pemmican for my dogs, 1 lb. each. But when I got to my sledge I could only see slight lumps in the snow, the dogs being completely covered up. So I had to shove the pemmican into the snow, just in front of their noses—having tried to push it into their tails first. . . .

WAGER — We cooked a thick pemmican, pea-flour and plasmon meal, drank a mug of tea and still felt desperately thirsty. Thirst became really bad as soon as one warmed up. We let the primus roar for a bit and managed to dry our blanket coats a little—some of the water vapour escaping out of the ventilator at the top of the tent, I suppose, but I fancy very little. The moment we put the primus out hoar-frost covered the walls.

The moon just after sunset was also setting and was dark pink through the blizzard. A good aurora helped us to put the final stones round our tent. Of recent nights other colours besides primrose and yellow, such as purple and red, have been visible at the lower edge of the aurora curtains.

October 31st

STEPHENSON — Got up at 4.30 a.m. and had breakfast—the usual, a plate of porridge, a biscuit and a drink of something. When I got out, it was still star-light night—but quite bright enough to see.

WAGER — Windless morning, and the existence or absence of wind colours one's whole outlook for the day. Again a few high cirrus which were pinked at dawn.

The day has been spent getting loads up Bugbear Bank. With seven of us working all day only five loads were got up. The block and tackle has been used every time. This makes it slow, but less tiring. My dogs are willing but weak, and old Federson has a badly swollen shoulder and is at present useless. Steve and I camped at the same place as last night. The others, except the backers-up, are at the top of Bugbear. My toe has again suffered from cold but I hope is not actually frost-bitten.

Wrote a letter to Dad suggesting what might be done with my insurance money if I fall irreparably into a crevasse—which is not very likely.

CHAPMAN — Lemon's dogs were left at the top of Bugbear for a few minutes today and broke into a bag of pemmican on the sledge, eating 25 lbs.

November 1st, Saturday

COURTAULD — Found that Milly had pupped in the night in spite of the experts' denial of the possibility. Somehow she had struggled out of her harness and made a little hole in the snow for herself. Mercayok had cut [his trace] and refused to be caught, so it left me with five dogs, only four of which were any good. Got stuck on all the little hummocks. Had to do most of the pulling. V. hard work. Took the loads about a mile short of the crevasses, going good and had a fine drive back to camp with empty sledges. . . .

Lemon's dogs ran away downhill with the wireless sledge, which overturned. It will be lucky if the wireless works when we reach the Ice Cap Station.

WAGER — My dog Federson has a festering wound on his shoulder which has produced a bad swelling. We tied him to the rocks, but we had only gone a few yards before he came stumbling after us, having bitten his trace. He had never bitten before but realised I suppose that he must hang on to old Sort at any price.

There was some sun and the going was better than last time we were here [with the first half of the loads], as snow had filled up a good deal of the hollows. However, the sledge tipped over three times. Had a quick lunch, sharing it with the other three [the supporting party], who now have very little food left. They expected to leave us three days ago.

My dogs, now four foxes and Sort, pull well but are not only few in number—the foxes are small. Passed their dump [Courtauld's and Chapman's] which was not quite on the usual route and got to the slope below the crevasses. Here Steve and the other two pitched our tent while Rymill and I went on to work out the way through the crevasses. This is most difficult country to steer an accurate course through because, with every different position of the sun, the shadows marking the undulations and crevasses change. Rymill went with great care probing to find out the size of every crevasse he went over. He is amazingly sound. As a matter of fact he had to turn back before we were through and Steve and I went back and worked fairly easily through them and over the hill till we could see into the next valley.

STEPHENSON — It is extraordinary what a feeling of comradeship can arise when roped together in such circumstances. One of us frequently fell through the snow up to our knees—but we discovered all the deep crevasses by probing and avoiding them. These bad ones only last about a half-mile. Then the going is fairly good to the Big Flag and the straight north-west route to the I.C.S. We flagged a way through the crevasses, then returned to our camp just as it was getting dark. We are up about 3,000 feet now, and get a wonderful view of the coast and fjords. Tonight it is a clear moonlight night and the snow has a very glossy surface of ice which makes it glitter most fantastically. . . . I hope my dogs behave better tonight. Last night they howled solidly for about an hour, and this morning I discovered five of them had bitten their traces. This means tying knots until I have time to splice, which only increases the complications of the usual tangle. They are jolly nice animals and usually pull well, but are quite capable of being the most maddening and heart-breaking creatures on earth. They have a habit of pulling well until they get to the top of a little rise. Then they sit down and wonder why you don't push the sledge on. Or else when you have just disentangled their traces they decide to have a fight and immediately get into a glorious muddle. It would be an exceptional man who did not lose his temper with his dogs some time or another. We were presented with another set of pups this morning which the supporting party will take back. [The puppies referred to by Courtauld.]

November 2nd, Sunday

WAGER — Steve and I had camped just below the crevasses some mile ahead of the other two tents. We had no alarm clock and did not awake till 5 a.m. Steve cooked and I got out first after breakfast. The morning was sunny and I hastily lashed skis and certain other odds and ends belonging to the others on my sledge and drove down to their camp. My dogs are pleasant creatures and on the whole intelligent, and without a track and no skill with a whip I drove pretty well straight there.

They had not got their tents down or sledges lashed so we had more than caught up the extra half-hour in bed. Freddie had worked out the loads. Mine with five dogs (Federson will have to return) is 300 lb. plus personal kit of both Steve and me. It includes tent, cooking things, and S.R. [sledging ration] box.

Hurriedly lashed loads after some argument as to amount. No one wants more than his share. By about ten o'clock a sledge had come up from the other camp with the supporting party from their mountain tent below Bugbear. With about six hands and I leading on forty feet of alpine rope we took one sledge through the crevasses. We could see a blizzard blowing on the ridge to the north and that to the south-west of us, and presently we were also in a blizzard. The fine powder snow was streaking along the surface of the snow, and on the whole our heads were out of the worst of it. This frequent powerful blizzard outwards from the Ice Cap must be an important way in which the snow falling on the Ice Cap is removed—perhaps as important as the slow flow of the ice itself. With the sun shining in our faces, the ice-crusted snow (called by skiers wind-crust) was blue, and the soft drifted snow was purple. The sun through the blizzard is a glorious orange. At present about half the surface of the snow is wind-crusted and will usually support a man's weight. The other half is soft drift snow often a foot thick. We have discarded boots, which will be taken back by the supporting party, and are wearing moccasins—except me who yesterday put on a fur boot because of a touch of frost-bite on my big toe. My boots were a little small and moreover never got a chance of recovering after both being completely immersed in a stream from the foot of the glacier. The supporters are not properly clothed nor have they had a proper amount of food, but are doing good work nevertheless. In the course of the day we got all the sledges just over the crevasses. Lemon especially had gone through up to his waist a time or so. He is not in good training and yet lights a cigarette at a halt even if a blizzard is blowing. Twice a sledge overturned over a crevasse, but with no damage.

Rymill, who had sent Cozens and Martin back a quarter of an hour before, had just left us with Federson, and we had just got all six teams moving, when a really nasty blizzard came up suddenly. We very much wanted to get into the shelter of the valley half a mile ahead, but it was impossible. The dogs could not possibly pull against the driving snow and we decided to pitch the tents at once. This was an awkward job in such a blizzard. All worked on one tent, half blinded by ice over the whole of one's face. Before the blizzard, the sunset and the moon together were making it comparatively light and I was enjoying the view of the mountains below the rising moon towards Angmagssalik. They were a glorious picture in whites and blues. But the blizzard not only blotted out all this but made it almost pitch black.

We got two tents up and decided that was enough. Ham came into our tent and Courtauld into Freddie's. The whole tent was full of kit-bags and rucksacks and us all covered in snow. We cooked a large pemmican and peaflour soup as we were. We could not afford anything more. Then with great care and cheerfulness we dusted everything we could, picked up the ground-sheet, shook it and gradually got our snow-free things and snow-free selves onto the dry ground-sheet. Then one at a time we got into our comfortable reindeer bags. It was a desperate squash, and it was very clear how stupid it would have been to have arranged to have three in a tent at this time of year as had seemed possible when Martin was going to come the whole way.

CHAPMAN — The supporting party had to go back to the Base today. They have stayed with us far longer than we expected and have helped us enormously.

November 3rd, Monday

WAGER — Blew all night but had good sleep. Freddie called to us to get up soon after dawn in case the wind dropped and we could go on. At the head end we were covered by snow from the hoar-frost formed from our breath on the walls of the tent and then shaken off by the wind.

We got out of our sacks, and in one corner of the tent pulled back the ground-sheet and cooked a very diluted mess of porridge and plasmon, all we had left of these things in our first sledging box. Still, it filled us a little and began to quench our thirst. Afterwards we had a cupful of lime juice with two lumps of sugar.

The blizzard was still blowing hard so we settled down and I wrote yesterday's diary and now am looking forward to reading.

Monday continued

It blew all day—we packed together. Ham was on his back with his knees up: my legs were bent but sideways under his, and Steve's also under, but usually straight. Read a little, then sang some of the songs in the *Week-end Book*. At 2.30 Freddie called out that one of us must get out and help find the dogs. So with windproofs on I crept out. Sunny but much driving snow. My dogs and sledge, in an eddy from Ham's, were deeply buried. Vixen and Sort were being held down deep into the snow by their traces. It took about an hour to free them and feed them—this 10 yards from the drift so that they would not be so deeply buried tomorrow. Vixen would not eat—despite the dog pemmican costing 25s. for a block of 7 lb. Each dog has 1 lb. a day. Although dog food for, I think, three weeks only has been allowed, it will cost £150 in dog food to get to the Ice Cap Station.

I took my windproof [smock] off outside, and this made me so anxious to get in that I bumped my forehead on a sledging box and made it bleed slightly.

We had supper of pemmican and pea-flour fairly early, about five o'clock, as we had had no lunch. Afterwards, while making eighteen traces out of string of the feeblest kind which a dog if it pulls with a jerk can break, we sang a selection of songs and sea-shanties to the amusement of the other tent.

November 4th, Tuesday

COURTAULD — Wind went down in the night and we rose at 2 a.m.—owing to a confusion of Greenwich and our time—to find a dark cloudy morning with only the faint light of a setting moon to light our work.

CHAPMAN — Wager was first outside and I asked him how light it was. I remember the laconic answer: "It's light enough to dig."

COURTAULD — It was not till eleven o'clock that we were ready to start. Weather for a moment fine. Our loads were heavy but the going was good and downhill for the first half-mile. We were not left in peace for long however. Soon the usual cold wind from the centre began to pipe up with snow. We slowly plodded our way and cursed our dogs uphill on the other side of the valley, and about 3 p.m. reached and got through the second crevasses. My sledge nearly went through. Wind increased with cold driving snow so we camped at sunset with the usual medley of flying and flapping tents and the cold whistling of this sickening wind.

November 5th, Wednesday

WAGER — For the first time I have been rather cold during the night. A blizzard blowing and therefore not called.

Monday's inactivity as a result of the blizzard was pleasant, coming as it did after a week of strenuousness. But today makes me think of what Freddie said yesterday to me. He was no doubt trying to counterbalance his usual optimism, but he thought a fair estimate of our rate of progress would be ten miles on days we could travel and probably only one travelling day in two. From the Big Flag which is now only one or two miles off it is 110 miles to the Ice Cap Station, i.e. we shall probably be another twenty-two days getting there. It really is foolish to be taking up food and wireless for that station in November. I am glad at present that the responsibility of the undertaking is Freddie's and not mine.

CHAPMAN — We must look at our position now. We have done ten miles in eleven days. Clearly we can only expect to travel one day in two, and thus seven miles per day will be our utmost limit. The weather will probably get worse as winter advances. We must expect thirty or forty more degrees of frost and the days are fast shortening: very soon we shall only have a few hours of daylight. The dogs are already showing signs of weakening.

Obviously some of the party must return. But who and how many? If we have to rely on the aeroplane, then the wireless, and Lemon to work it, must go on. We have only had one flying day in ten so far, but this may change when the sea is completely frozen over. We started a new ration box today and were bitterly disappointed to find that the chocolate, the only thing that makes life worth living on a journey like this, had been taken out.

WAGER — 7 p.m. I have decided in the case of my personal diary, at any rate at present, that though describing things under the date they happened I will put after them the date they were written. Steve always writes his diary in the evening of the day, which is a desideratum to which I wish I could attain.

COURTAULD — Got out about 3 p.m. to feed the dogs. Wind furious. Could only walk against it with face turned away. Most of the dogs were buried in the snow with only their noses out. Some of them did not seem to want their pemmican.

WAGER — We bring in two pans of snow, boil it and take it in some form. The most of it leaves us in our breath and condenses on our bags near our mouth or on the tent walls above, from whence it is shaken onto us as snow. Just while the primus is burning, most of the hoar-frost on the walls melts exactly down to the level of the primus. To lower this level we are now putting the primus on the floor instead of on the ration box.

The sun has been shining all day, and as we peeped out at sunset there was a magnificent red glow in the south-west with red and grey horizontal cloud bands.

I read some of D. Osborne's letters and Steve has not even read.

STEPHENSON — Neither man nor dog could hope to travel in this wind. We are allowed two ration boxes per tent on this journey out— which is normally a two weeks' journey. On half rations we can live for a month. We have got plenty of food with us, but to break into that means breaking into the supply for the I.C.S.—which at the moment will last until the middle of March. If the aeroplanes don't succeed in relieving people it looks as if Ham and I will have to stay there all winter—as travelling in this is pretty well impossible.

November 6th, Thursday

WAGER — Blizzard still blowing and I have not stirred out of the tent all day. In the night there was a calm and all the dogs howled miserably. I think Unalite was near our tent, howling for her puppies and starting all the others. However, they are having a poor time and one can scarcely blame them— though in the night if one could have gone out without much dressing up I should have beaten them hard. I do not know for how long there was calm, but it started to blow again before 4 a.m., the time we should have otherwise got up.

I ate a little raw pemmican at about seven o'clock and read the *Week-end Book* poems. Steve turned out at 10.30 and got the new sledging box. We had packed things in bags and had half-melted snow for porridge when the primus gave out—no paraffin. We had to have one biscuit and ⅛ lb. chocolate instead.

Mended my trousers and extended the opening of my windproof. Then Freddie came in. They had been talking over plans and decided that the dog food would run out if this kind of blizzard continues to be so frequent. He is proposing that after a few days Hampton, Courtauld and self return while the others push on. Hampton's returning to make use of aeroplane if necessary. Steve is going on to find their position if they lose the flags. Steve and Lemon are to do a spell at the Ice Cap together.

CHAPMAN — In the evening the gale became ghastly—well over 100 m.p.h. It must have felt rather like this being under shell-fire during the war.

November 7th, Friday

WAGER — I slept little of the first part of the night, and about midnight as I should guess I got up and ate my day's ration of chocolate. The gale still increased and I took out my windproof top from my rucksack and put it in my sleeping-bag. My wet windproof trousers I put under my pillow, and I then put my glove string round my neck and tied my fur boots to it. Duffles I also put in my fur bag. I suggested to Steve that the tent might go, and did he know where his windproofs were? But he was too sleepy to care.

COURTAULD — We slept in our clothes and prayed that the tent could stay up. One dreads to think what it would be like were it to blow away. It was a terrifying experience. Both the tents had part

61

of their outsides lifted but luckily not carried away. Towards morning it moderated slightly, leaving us thankful, if cold and wet.

WAGER — We seem about one to two miles from what I judge to be the Big Flag.

About 2 p.m. one of my dogs, which I had seen to be half buried, howled so piteously that I went out again and cut her trace and dug her out with a shovel. I fed all the dogs on pemmican and dog fat, and dug out and cut the traces of those buried or nearly buried.

COURTAULD — A further discovery of chocolate missing from a sledging box today. At some time or other some friend must have unscrewed as many boxes as he could get hold of, taken out the chocolate and screwed them up again.

November 8th, Saturday

COURTAULD — A fairly calm cloudy morning. Turned out at daybreak. Temp. quite mild, minus 2 degrees. Sledges, dogs and traces were in horrible mess after the gale. All my dogs had cut their traces as well as the lash line in several places. Everything was buried under the usual feet of snow and frozen urine.

WAGER — There was dense cloud over the sea and less dense over us. As my sledge and dogs were deeper in than other people's—I was this time in the lee of Freddie's—it was a good thing I was out early. I am learning wisdom only slowly despite the laboriousness of the business of digging out sledge and traces. We were not ready to start till 11.30, but going was good and our speed about 2 m.p.h., I should guess.

Freddie picked out a flag with his glasses before we left camp. I saw a flag beyond and a larger one which for some time I took for Gino's party. We reached a smaller flag first but then quickly the Big Flag. (A tin of meat for supper!) I had about 100 lb. less load and my dogs could just pull it, making travelling far pleasanter than last time. Still they are slow and I have continually to say "Dammer."

I suggested to Freddie returning in relays of two, and he was taken with the idea. I shall either go back with Courtauld first or on with Steve to the end, and I suspect the former.

Flags are at half-mile intervals, and towards dusk we missed one and are camping not for certain on the route. Already the Ice Cap is becoming a featureless mass.

CHAPMAN — It is absolutely essential for us to keep on the line of flags. Once we miss them we lose hope of finding the Station, as position-finding may be impossible in the cold we shall get later, and when the sun will only just clear the horizon. I am wearing three pairs of socks and three pairs of blanket shoes and fur boots, pants and vest, sweater, blanket trousers and coat, windproof trousers and coat, canvas leggings to keep the snow out, two pairs of wool mits and wolf-skin mits, wool helmet and windproof hood.

November 9th, Sunday

WAGER — 10 a.m. A wind got up in the night. It seems from north or even north-east quarter. The wind was too strong for us to go on.

PORTRAIT OF AN ICE CAP

It will be most exciting to have Wegener's account of his meteorological expedition to the Ice Cap, based on the same year of weather that we are experiencing. [Professor Wegener's German expedition—of which more later—was establishing an Ice Cap Station three hundred miles further north.]

Yesterday I felt more friendly towards the dogs. They pulled well and the load was such that they could just manage it. They even started more or less simultaneous with my efforts at waggling the sledge sideways and thus giving it a start. The team consists of four of the fox family—one had to be left behind at the Base because of a sore foot. The leader, Kernek —meaning black—is not foxy in colour, is lop-eared and friendly. In his friendliness he often makes a bad tangle of the traces. He is also very friendly with his team, especially with Bob—Angekok—who is one of the prettiest dogs I have seen. Bob has long matted hair and was called Bob by Freddie who had forgotten his name and was reminded of a Shap dog of that name. Plain is called plain because he has not got light spots over his eyes. He is rather characterless. The Vixen is very small but pulls well. She is very timid and not handsome.

Sort does not belong to the fox family and is miserably alone now Federson has gone back. He is bigger than the foxes and in his own family would be a splendid dog but tends now to sulk and whine. Yesterday he was sick as a result of eating too much pemmican. Due to dogs cutting their own traces or having to have them cut to let them keep above the

Heavy going near the coast

Sledge dogs

drifting snow a considerable amount of pemmican has been stolen by the dogs eating through the calico bags. It is the shortage of dog pemmican and not of man rations which will necessitate some of us turning before we reach the Ice Cap Station.

Freddie cut off Hinks's tail the day before yesterday. It was stuck in the snow and he thought he was only cutting the hair. Yesterday morning he discovered the other half of the tail in the snow. The dog had not shown any signs of discomfort.

Four of Steve's fingers have now got blisters on the ends due to a touch of frost-bite. My big toe also remains with a blister which never feels really comfortable.

We had one hail from Freddie at 2 p.m. telling us to pass on to Ham and Courtauld that it was their turn to feed the dogs.

Have not read much—one or two poems in the *Week-end Book*. I am getting better at reading poetry but also at doing nothing. In the early morning I tend to think a little too hard about the present plans or to regret that I am not getting on with geology, but after breakfast I feel better and think aimlessly about things in England or the strange meteorology here, or about Dorothy Osborne whose love letters I am reading. When I get a chance I think aloud to Steve or we discuss things and people at Cambridge. Often too we sing snatches—seldom the whole of a song.

STEPHENSON — Reading is a little difficult as it is cold for the hands and the pages get wet with the hoar-frost blown off the tent. Nevertheless I am going to read some of *The Manhood of the Master* before retiring—the present condition helping one to realise the truth of it all. It is a wonderful opportunity to get outside the world with such a book as this. One realises more and more what things are important and necessary and what a lot of time is spent in the trifling things of life. I am sure these days of physical idleness are good for one. An hour or two's solid thought whilst bound down by the elements reveals to one the absolute helplessness of man against such forces and how much he is dependent on outside help.

November 10th, Monday

STEPHENSON — So revolves the kaleidoscope of chance! This morning I rose all eagerness to get a bit nearer my destination [the Ice Cap Station]. Tonight I am going to bed having made preparations to leave the rest tomorrow and return to the Base with Ham and Lemon.

CHAPMAN — Fifteen miles, fifteen days: what a hope! 48 degrees of frost in the night. Visibility bad: diffused light and slight snow. Suddenly saw a small moving object in the distance away to the left. A dog? A bear? It proved to be Watkins and Scott returning from their journey.

WAGER — They appeared as dots away to the south of us, off the Ice Cap Station route. Had we or they been fifteen minutes earlier or later we should not have met. They had done only a fraction of what they had hoped. Dogs and blizzards had interfered. Gino was loth to discuss any plans for us but agreed to leaving the wireless. He thought we should have great difficulties in making the I.C.S. and several times said we must abandon it if necessary and eat our dogs if necessary. However, before leaving them, it was practically decided that Freddie, Courtauld and I should go on and that Courtauld and I should be left. What a rapid change of plans. Only this morning Freddie had definitely told us that Courtauld and I would return on the next travelling day and Ham and Steve would go on. Gino's idea was that Ham was needed for the aeroplanes.

While talking, Steve's nose and part of his face went white—the beginning of frost-bite. But it is perfectly right tonight.

Made only about six miles today, and the snow is getting worse—softer and also more blown into sastrugi [wind drifts].

Had a full-ration dinner which we enjoyed far more than we expected.

Soupe à la 'wild pemmican'
Bœuf de chien sauté
Porridge and Plasmon with margarine
Horlicks
Chocolate
Strong Lemon.

CHAPTER VI

Chapman, Courtauld and Wager

November 11*th, Tuesday*

CHAPMAN — Dumped wireless and seven ration boxes at Flag 56. Spoiling the Egyptian wasn't in it. We took [from Stephenson, Lemon and Hampton who were returning to the Base] the three best teams of seven dogs each that we could make up. We also took the best of everything they had, sledges, clothes, books, whips. Got away by 11.30. We have arranged to have a dinner in London next Armistice Day. I really felt quite sad to see them turn their sledges in the other direction and leave us. We have arranged a code for the aeroplane. An 'X' on the snow if landing impossible, and an 'O' if possible.

Courtauld came into our tent this morning and suggested that he should stay alone at the Ice Cap Station. He stressed what has been worrying me, namely that we shall take so long to reach the Station that we shan't have enough supplies to leave for two people. Furthermore, the bad weather, having started so early, may continue till February and even over March, so that no sledge party could come up and the aeroplane could not land.

WAGER — Steve let me have pants and vest, brush, books, paper, pencils, and flashlight.

Forgot the two-minute silence.

CHAPMAN — We now go on for a mile [by cyclo-meter sledge wheel] after we miss a flag in the gathering darkness. It is an awful strain gazing into the void looking for flags. You have simply no idea what focus to use as there is nothing to focus on. We thought we saw a big dark-coloured object in the distance today but found it was a small piece of black paper only ten yards away.

Tried all three in one tent tonight, but under these conditions it is impracticable. There is so much ice frozen onto the inside of the tent below the primus-level that the tent is minute. With three of us we are always touching the tent wall, which lets loose showers of rime onto us. My watch froze up today and won't start again.

November 12th, Wednesday

WAGER — I in tent by myself. This resulted in a strange experience. After supper I had been com-pletely fumed by the cooking in the tent—candle burnt low or even would not burn. Then I had to go out into a mild blizzard. Filled pots with snow, felt queerish and almost fainted by exertion getting through doors. Then matches would not light, nor another box I searched out, but at last went for Marbles box and they lit. Got into bed as soon as I could. Soon felt better and so got out again and added dry pair of socks, trousers and pyjama-jacket. Then felt cheerful enough to write diary.

CHAPMAN — Several flags so far have been buried and the bunting is usually torn to shreds. Very often too they are obscured by drifts and we can't see them till we are fifty yards away. So accurate steering is essential.

Wager came over and had supper with us. We didn't take enough primus prickers from the other people and I had to use the second-hand off my watch today after trying all sorts of other implements. But Wager is a wizard with the primus and has made it work. The fumes in the tent are very bad. Our pipes would not light today.

November 13th, Thursday

COURTAULD — Came on to blow in the night and continued all day. No travel possible.

WAGER — After breakfast I roasted the burner of the primus that was choked and tapped it and sucked it and at last made it go. Rather uncomfortable in the tent. Freddie read some of the things in Palgrave.

Got out about 1 p.m. Fed dogs. Sun shining through blizzard.

The Ice Cap is now an almost flat plane of snow with a circular horizon as at sea. Cloud shadows show up grey. In detail the surface is crossed by drifts of snow showing a wind from the north-north-west to east. Yesterday the wind from the north-east with the accompanying precipitation was producing smaller drifts across the main ones, and the modelling was often beautiful.

Last night I gave reasons for my view that I ought to stay at the Ice Cap Station with August. I rather think that if we get sufficient food there I shall be staying.

CHAPMAN, COURTAULD AND WAGER

We have eaten nearly the whole of our chocolate ration for the next eight days.

November 14th, Friday

COURTAULD — Still blowing with thick drift. Lay up all day. Went out to feed the dogs at two o'clock. Temp. minus 19 degrees. Wind force 6, most unpleasant. Freddie read *Troilus and Cressida* in the evening.

WAGER — Wind dying down. I hope we can travel tomorrow. Nevertheless I have enjoyed today and am now going to read more of Dorothy Osborne's letters.

November 15th, Saturday (Flag 90)

COURTAULD — Wind dropped in early morning so we decided to travel. Sledges, dogs, tents, kit all buried under snow. It was after noon before we were away. Cold work getting things in order. Temp. 9 a.m. minus 20 degrees. Min. in night minus 32 degrees. Cold north-west wind force 4. Drifts very bad. Sledges overturned every few yards. Freddie's sledge showed signs of breaking up so we camped about four o'clock. Decided to lighten his sledge and only take on enough food for one man—self—at Ice Cap. We shall therefore only take four instead of fourteen boxes there. It looks as if the useful result of this journey will be small indeed. Had a tin of sardines for supper. V.G.

WAGER — It was a magnificent day. One or two wisps of cirrus over the Ice Cap, but beyond in the direction of Sermilik Fjord and the Base low cloud

71

could be seen apparently struggling to come up onto the Ice Cap against the wind. A small grey-white sugar loaf to the north Freddie said was Mt. Forel. Just before we left the camp it had completely disappeared. In fact it had only been showing due to refraction effect.

The brilliant sun produced dark shadows in the drifts and made it difficult to see the flags. The drift in the eddy of my tent was four to five feet high and stretched forty to fifty yards. The going was not good as there were occasional hard upstanding drifts, very finely modelled and of the consistency almost of chalk, but breaking more easily. Even when small these would turn over a sledge as they were so hard.

Our late start and slow progress because of overturns, and our early stop because Freddie's sledge smashed up more, resulted in our doing only two miles. This is pretty miserable when one considers all the packing, taking down of half-buried tents, digging out sledges and traces, untangling traces, lashing loads that was necessary before we got off—and this in a cold wind so that one could not think clearly or do things properly. Then after two miles all the business of unloading and pitching tents.

I am still in a tent by myself. I feel that this should rotate though not necessary every day. However it is really reasonable enough as Freddie and August will have to discuss what to take on. It was August's idea to stay on by himself and he very much wanted to do so. In fact my insistence on staying he has always attempted to dispute, so that there is no question of who stays at the Ice Cap Station. I am most sorry that I am not.

CHAPMAN — So many black shadows cast by the drifts that it's hard to see the flags. Wind terribly cold. Our noses got frost-bitten often today, but as long as your hands don't go too you can thaw your nose out.

November 16th, Sunday (*Flag* 90)

COURTAULD — Another gale got up in the night and again we lay up all day, indulging in alternations of cooking and reading aloud. The result of these were oatcakes of a sort, toffee, peas, the whole of *King John*, sundry sonnets and the whole of *Alice in Wonderland*. Wind dropped at sunset but rose after dark.

WAGER — During the night (11 p.m.) I awoke to find the wind so bad that I lit a candle to see if the tent was moving much. It was however quite rigid and I slept well till 8 a.m. Having the previous evening turned my sack inside out and shaken out the hoar-frost and then dried it somewhat, I was comfortably warm.

I have thoroughly enjoyed the day. It began by gloomy thoughts occasioned by the blizzard preventing us from travelling, and the thought that we have been three whole weeks now and only got twenty or twenty-five miles from the Big Flag. We have between eighty and ninety miles to do and the blizzards will only let us travel two or three days a week.

I spent the morning thinking over the tectonics of the dyke and plateau basalt formation about Kangerd-lugssuaq. A scheme beginning with thinning of the sial by tension fits the facts pretty well.

PORTRAIT OF AN ICE CAP

Have finished *Twelfth Night*. Brushed my teeth although they did not really need it, and now—7 p.m.—intend to read for another hour. Have had the primus going all day except for about an hour. The moment I let it out the walls freeze and my breath begins to form hoar-frost on them. One fill of paraffin—I should guess less than one quart—seems to last about eight hours.

The wind is still pretty strong. I hope we can travel tomorrow—despite the pleasures of lying up—or when shall we get there?

November 17th, Monday

CHAPMAN — Blizzard continues. Enjoyed today vastly. Though it's irksome not to be able to get on: yet we can't move, and there it is. There is a consoling inevitability about it. The contrast of the companionship and comparative comfort of a warm tent to straining along in the cold, cursing your dogs, is immense. Read *Master of Ballantrae* today and started *Treasure Island* again.

WAGER — Spent most of day thinking over geological things. As I shall not be at the Ice Cap to work through the list of things to be done which I drew up two days ago, I am making a start with them now. Have been considering the intrusions and their relation to tectonics. Have also made a beginning with a classification of the metamorphic types along the coast.

Have learnt: D. G. Rossetti's *The Woodspurge* and *O Mistress Mine, where art thou roaming?*

Finished *King John*—a first-rate play. Also dried my sack again. Freddie's primus has got stopped up and tomorrow I am to prepare cocoa for their breakfast.

November 18*th, Tuesday*

CHAPMAN — Lay up all day again. Two miles in five days. It looks as if we shall have to go on till the dog food is finished, then kill the weaker dogs as food for the others, then—if we find the Station—collect Bingham and D'Aeth and man-haul back.

The snow is whistling along with a continuous droning sound. Much troubled by sores, which have gone septic, caused by my trousers rubbing.

COURTAULD — Wind increased in the night to gale force and blew all day. I had to feed the dogs. Could hardly stand up in the wind. Only got about with the utmost difficulty.

WAGER — Could not shout across the six yards separating the two tents to hear whether their primus was going. All day there has been the incessant roar and flapping of which by now—7 p.m.—I am not a little tired. The air when I looked out was simply a cloud of snow.

Spent several enjoyable hours thinking over geological things. Have also read *Richard II*, but now I am a little weary of the day. I think I have also eaten a little too much pemmican.

November 19*th, Wednesday*

COURTAULD — A fine day at last. Got packed late after lying up so long, and of course found not a single trace on any dog. Although they had been set free from the sledge they had all chewed them off. Freddie's sledge was incapable of more than a half load, so Wager and I were loaded pretty heavily. We somehow found some old bits of string and knotted up seven traces. Then we started. We hadn't been going a quarter of a mile before all the sledges were over. The surface was alternatively knife edge as hard as concrete or soft snow. The snow drifts lay in islands and always the dogs seemed to make straight for them and plough through the middle while we ran cursing beside our sledges, now pulling now pushing, to prevent them upsetting. About every ten minutes the sledge would upset and the dogs would sit down with a satisfied look while we turned it right side up.

Every time this happened it made the sledge weaker and nearer breaking point. The sun set and all the western sky glowed, but still we tried to get on. The stars came out and found us at it as hard and struggling as vainly as ever. At last Freddie's sledge broke down completely so we were forced to camp having made a bare five miles.

WAGER — Two things have been in my mind. One—somebody's remark before we left the wireless that this will be an epic journey—a damned silly one I think in lots of ways. And secondly Courtauld's remark today that he felt optimistic about our journey. What I feel is wanted is a little sober calculation of probabilities so that we make a more determined effort to increase our speed.

CHAPMAN, COURTAULD AND WAGER

November 20th, Thursday

COURTAULD — Found to our surprise that we had done fifty-six miles from the Big Flag, leaving sixty-two to go.

CHAPMAN — Worst day I've ever had. With the sores in my fork and frost-bitten toes each step is agony. Several times I just couldn't go on and had to sit down for a few minutes.

We went on a long way after sunset today. I found I could keep a good enough line by steering on the stars. We used the lowest star of the 'handle' of the Great Bear. Luckily we passed within ten yards of the flags and so could see them.

WAGER — My dogs pulling well. New trace method seems good. Freddie talking of killing two of his to save dog food. August's ran away just as he was about to tie them on to the sledge and went a mile or so. They came to us after we had started.

November 21st, Friday

COURTAULD — Another day even worse than yesterday. After Freddie's sledge had again been repaired, we got away about ten. Traces in hopeless state, constantly breaking. Drifts awful, hard concrete ridges with soft deep snow in between. Sledge over-turning all the while. Mt. Forel not visible in the morning but later in the day was refracted up with all its range of mountains in a most fantastic way. Freddie again having a bad time with his frost-bite and fork. My dogs got worse and worse. Tiss being about to pup makes things more difficult. Sledge beginning to pass out.

Camped at last thoroughly worn out after doing six miles. Now are half-way from the Big Flag. The continued effort at this height (6 or 7,000 feet), struggling through the snow without snow shoes (which the dogs have eaten), keeping one's sledge upright, cursing one's dogs and continually restarting, tires one out almost beyond endurance.

WAGER — When we stopped we killed the poor little bitch of Freddie's team who had the puppies under the hut at the Base. She was not worth her pemmican, and seemed half comatose.

Had a third of a tin of strawberry jam, half frozen, at supper-time. I have never known anything taste so glorious.

Freddie in all seriousness said that I was even-tempered both with the others and the dogs. It is not true but rather a pleasant impression to be creating. But Freddie is a bit of a flatterer at times.

November 22nd, Saturday (*Flag* 124)

WAGER — When I dug out my sledge I discovered the back half of one runner completely squashed because the iron angle bars on the back three uprights had come adrift. I began at once to do what Ham and I had done for another sledge at the camp beyond the first crevasses. It became gradually clear that to do the job well would take all day, and it was decided to give the day up to this and getting the other sledges quite ready to start. I worked hard till 3.30 cutting notches in three bits of ash and binding them on. I also tried to tighten the thongs by driving in wedges. The sledge will stick now in soft snow, and I am doubtful how she will behave to oblique drifts as she is now more rigid. The two ends I could do by drawing them into tent, but the middle had to be done outside. Altogether a cold job and my hands are blistered where the knife rubbed them most.

Some cloud about all day and slight to moderate wind, but I have scarcely had time to notice these things.

Have just gone through my kit to sort things and found tobacco. Have had a pipe but it gave me little satisfaction. Have now three hours to read and think and have supper.

Freddie seems fitter and we are promising ourselves a record mileage tomorrow. Tomorrow begins our fifth week.

November 23rd, Sunday (*Flag* 136)

CHAPMAN — 57 degrees of frost all day. We are all feeling the height and cold. It is a tremendous effort to dress and lash up: we just lie back and pant after any exertion. Sun rose at 8.30. A mile an hour is our maximum speed. Did six miles. Flags are very battered here and hard to pick out.

WAGER — A new type made its appearance today, namely softish snow—neither powder as filling hollows, nor chalky as in wind drifts. This formed rounded mounds and ridges and was good going but very rare, and the size of the ridges was usually only some ten yards. Again greatly admired the cuspate form of the chalky wind drifts. But these attractive drifts have been an awful nuisance for the sledge. I have upset most today, probably five times, and I have required assistance to prevent upsetting a dozen times.

Have not felt quite so fit as usually and I have taken a half-spoonful of cod-liver oil—but I don't really believe I have a vitamin shortage, just sick of pemmican. It is a month from the day that we started and I am going to put on a clean pair of thick pants and vest underneath everything. I shall not remove anything—they will merely go up one. May be able to keep warmer at nights with a more fluffy and less sweated layer next me.

Read some of *Romeo and Juliet* and thought it excellent, and as we stopped early I shall have another half-hour at it tonight.

November 24th, Monday

WAGER — Cirrus clouds were covering about half the sky and it was a fine sunrise. Just before they were pinked, the shapely wisps of cirrus were white on a sky of most unusual blue.

At a temporary breakdown of a sledge I again enquired if there was nothing we could leave behind. We have still fifty miles to go, and all the way back, and the sledges are really falling to bits with the rough going.

Exertion of any kind is two or three times as exhausting as usual and I am reminded of the half-empty cod-liver oil bottle I opened yesterday. It is in

A calm
evening

a Mousseux bottle and it went off like champagne when I uncorked it. It had not been opened since the Base—6,000 feet below us. But I think the cold also has something to do with our getting out of breath.

COURTAULD — We had only done two miles by lunch-time, and getting up to start again after our ten-minute lunch I found Tiss had produced a pup.

Impossible to do anything with it or keep it warm. After this, far from being distressed, she pulled like the best of them until an hour later when she began to scrape a hole to have another. During one of the halts to right Wager's sledge she produced it. At last my sledge upset in a bad place and the wind was beginning to cause a bad drift, so we camped. Tiss soon produced a third, so I made her as comfortable as possible with ration boxes and left her to do her best.

November 25th, Tuesday (Flag 143)

COURTAULD — Lay up all day. Wind strong in early morning, increased to gale force after noon.

WAGER — At times I am convinced my sack which I am sitting on is moving. But it is either the sudden back and forth movements of the air in the tent or illusion. Freddie fed the dogs and said it was minus 25 degrees. When I had the door open to give him Shakespeare and paraffin, and receive candle, *Kidnapped* and cigarettes, the whole air was full of snow. It has been unpleasant in the tent. Nose cold and hoar-frost dropping off the walls and laying a white coat everywhere. Food too is a little dull for off days, though good enough when travelling.

I have thought over geological things and possible future journeys now that the sledges are mostly broken and the going is so bad on the inland ice. I should like to hear Gino's present plans.

Have begun *Kidnapped*.

November 26th, Wednesday (*Flag* 143)

CHAPMAN — Lay up. Read *Cymbeline*, then started *Forsyte Saga*. Sledges falling to bits: what can we do? Dogs prowling round tent all evening.

WAGER — Really high wind during the night. It began to die down in the morning and is now a dead calm, bringing with it relief from the incessant flapping and making the tent much warmer.

At 1 p.m. I went out and fed the dogs. Clear sky but still enough wind to make a moderate amount of blowing snow. All Tiss's puppies had gone.

November 27th, Thursday (*Flag* 153)

WAGER — Snowing gently and little or no wind when we got out at 8 a.m. Reason late was that it was so dark. Seemed very warm partly because there was no wind, but temp. was relatively high, being minus 5 degrees F. We all had some patching to do on our sledges and did not start till 11.15. Impossible to see what we were coming to, though flags could often be seen half-mile off. Two to three inches of powder snow covered the other varieties. And as there were no shadows, but usually mist or snow, one generally seemed to be going on, over and in cotton-wool. Sledges overturned a good bit, but on the whole the going was good. Being warmer we were more cheerful and got out of breath, I think, less. Freddie's frost-bitten toe is on the whole getting worse, but his fork and himself better. Managed to do four and a half miles.

My dogs have all a decided character of their own which I am gradually learning. Augut, who is the boss dog, is smallish, horribly pushing and pretty intelligent. Coco—white, I think—is old and at present is rather pathetic because his harness was put on badly and badly fitted and he has sores as a result. Yet he pulls hard, and if the harness hurts particularly looks round pathetically at me. The other dogs are mostly very kind to him and lick his sores. Bruno really belongs to another team of which Snaps is also a member. He, I think, is old and has the sense which should result. He has little to do with the other dogs, in fact is stand-offish, whether at the Base or here. But at the Base he always expects human beings to fuss over him. He pulls pretty well but is getting thin now. Sukuluk —yellow and fattish still—lacks guts and is rather effeminate. He is good looking and whines very easily. I thought him very stupid about learning the meaning of "Illy" and "Yiuk" ["Right" and "Left"] but on the whole he is showing up better now. Kernek— black—seems still very fit and cheerful and jumps, putting a lot into it at the start. But he slacks some-times, especially if he can get his leg over another dog's trace as a sort of excuse. Besides these are the two Angmagssalik dogs. Capek is now squabbling with all the other dogs and is fast becoming the boss dog.

He is big and fit—partly because the others had only just come back from a journey—and he is absolutely fearless. He pulls well, sometimes very well. Salik, called by Lemon Angel—but the name when actually on a sledge journey does not always seem appropriate —shows up less well than at the Base. There he was always trotting about with Capek, and while Capek would not come near, Salik would come up to one and even start on walks with me. He pulls pretty well but is not nearly as fit as Capek and has less general go. Here he tends to be rather quiet.

Freddie is I think pretty tired of this trip. He had only just come back from one. But so are we all, I fancy.

November 28th, Friday

WAGER — I spent a feeble night. My sack and clothes were wet because of the high temperature and calm. The dogs were pottering about all night. Some of the wretches came and began to tear the tent, and I frightened them off. At twelve o'clock I awoke and heard them tearing the tent again, so got up and opened the door but found that the dog responsible had gone off. I wasted ten minutes getting cold but could not decide which dog it was. I was now cold and wet and could not sleep for a long time. Then I was awakened again by tearing—some dog was solemnly tearing the flap, on which the snow is put, into strips. It was very important that this kind of destruction should be stopped, and I looked out again. Capek was standing near and I believed he was responsible. Again

I was long in getting to sleep, so when called at 6 a.m. I did not feel in very good form.

Snow and a little wind. Some two or three inches must have fallen in the night. I noticed that the snow was in single crystals, usually very beautifully star-shaped in three dimensions. But perhaps one-fifth are star-shaped in two dimensions only. Very warm, plus 3 degrees F., and mist and snow made visibility poor.

I and Freddie beat Capek and then Kernek, who I believed had eaten my traces last night in the dusk. It was most exhausting and I had to sit down for a moment after the beating. I believe Kernek was guiltless and Tiss [Courtauld's bitch] got hold of my traces and began eating them. She might be mistaken for Kernek easily in the dark.

We are now thirty-eight miles from the Ice Cap Station—as far as from Hebden Bridge to Arncliffe. Though it means very little, I am always thinking of distances in terms of Arncliffe walks.

November 29th, *Saturday* (*Flag* 169)

COURTAULD — Wind blowing strong north-east all night. During the day it was back to west-north-west. Strong at evening with hard driving snow. Had an awful day getting through deep snow over knee-deep in places. Did four miles. Dogs could hardly get sledges along.

CHAPMAN — Dogs tore open a kit-bag last night and went off with a pair of binoculars, eating the leather case.

PORTRAIT OF AN ICE CAP

November 30th, Sunday

COURTAULD — Weather quiet and mostly over-cast with occasional snow squalls from north-west. Made a very good day and broke all records. Very thick in early morning with cold wind and driving snow. So could not see flags. After lashing up the sledges we set off in different directions and eventually found a flag about a quarter-mile off. Started at eleven with clearing sky and improving visibility. Going good. At noon the sun came out for a moment with two uprights of a bow about fifteen degrees from it, probably caused by slight snow drift. Sun nowadays is only above the horizon for an hour or two and of course is too low to give any heat. It looks quite nice however. Made good going, being able to sit on our sledges most of the time for the first time since leaving the Base. As there was a certain amount of moon we were able to carry on after dark. Camped about 7 p.m. having done twelve and a half miles. Celebrated by having full rations. If only we can have these conditions for a couple more days we shall be there.

CHAPTER VII

D'Aeth, Bingham—
and the Last Few Miles

ON November 30th, when Courtauld made the last quoted entry, Flight-Lieutenant D'Aeth and Surgeon-Lieutenant Bingham had been alone at the Ice Cap Station for eight weeks. They had expected to be relieved within five weeks, for as soon as Rymill's party got back to the Base they were to send up Lemon and Hampton with the wireless transmitting set. By summer experience, five weeks were amply sufficient for the double journey.

On October 30th, Doc Bingham was already writing: "Hope to see the relieving party some time about this day week." It was now November 30th, and still they had not come.

Doc and Jimmy D'Aeth, efficiently and with the sense of routine which comes of Service life, had done their observations and kept their Station in order. For recreation they had read, smoked, talked and played cards. They had made a number of neat improvements for the comfort of the tent. But of course they knew nothing about the changes to the plans, and since the winds were less strong on the highest part of the Ice Cap, where these originated, they did not appreciate the full fury of the weather further out, where the air was flowing downhill at its maximum velocity.

The wind, none the less, had been their constant enemy. They meant to hand over the Station in perfect order to the relieving party. But the wind ate away their snow walls and filled the courtyard with drift.

I will quote extracts from Bingham's diary, starting on November 11th—when the relief party were actually more than a hundred miles away.

Armistice Day

BINGHAM — Did a big day's work on the courtyard. . . . Hope no more drifts until the relief party arrive. Absolute calm all day for first time.

November 14th

Cleared out drifts in the compound and buildings. Walked a short way out along the flags to clear them. Judging by the intense cold on one's face caused by the wind and low temperature I am very sorry for the relief party coming up. No wonder they are behind time.

November 15th

Rather a nice day with good visibility. Thought we saw the relieving party in the distance, but a mirage made it difficult. Possibly they may arrive tomorrow . . . Temperature at 7 p.m. was minus 51·5 degrees and at 10 p.m. minus 19 degrees.

Opened 4 gallons of paraffin.

November 16th

. . . We now examine the back trail with glasses when doing the observations, but with no result.

THE LAST FEW MILES

November 17th

Good travelling day. Temperature at 10 p.m. plus 4 degrees F.

November 18th

Beastly day! High wind with no visibility. . . . Everything drifting up. Opened new ration box.

November 19th

Nice day and we got a lot of clearing done outside. Still no sign of relief party arriving, so we should get the whole place cleared before their arrival. . . . Yesterday gale had eaten away parts of our walls in a most peculiar fashion so that they were very thin and looked rotten. . . .

November 23rd

Left the Base ten weeks ago. Nice calm clear day but no sign of the relieving party. Walked down the flags a short way to clear them. . . .

November 25th

Blowing a stiff gale outside. Everything drifting up fast. The entrance to our tunnel which we cleared this morning is already blocked again. The tent is practically steady, but even with the snow house round it and a layer of drift snow in places feet thick all over it, the buffeting of the wind is quite alarming. Am not fancying the job of doing the 10 p.m. observations. Sorry for the fellows down the trail if they are getting this gale.

PORTRAIT OF AN ICE CAP

November 26th

. . . Behind the hut and snow houses a weak part of the wall had been blown through and an enormous drift formed, filling the whole space, and nearly as high as the tent. Ashpit now a mountain. . . .

Opened 4 gallons of paraffin.

November 27th

Wind got up in the night from a new direction and undid all our yesterday's work. . . . Got a lot done outside, clearing away snow and making wooden trapdoors for the entrances. . . .

November 28th

Another beastly day. . . .

November 29th

. . . When doing 7 a.m. observations I had to dig my way out and then mountaineer to get out of the courtyard, which was a most disheartening sight. Started to clear courtyard. . . .

November 30th

. . . Experienced an optical illusion this morning—thought the bits of paper on the snow about forty yards off were the relief party about two miles away. . . . Have two unopened ration boxes left as yet, besides some tins of pemmican and butter. Thoroughly tired of pemmican and hope the relief party have some meat of some sort.

·   ·   ·   ·   ·

THE LAST FEW MILES

[Courtauld's diary completes the account of the journey to the Station.]

December 1st to 4th

COURTAULD — The last few days have been such a mixture of despair and bliss, apprehension and contentment that there has been no time or, when there has been time, there has been no mood for writing them down.

For a further three days we were blessed with the best weather and travelling conditions we had struck the whole journey. On Monday after a late start we did about ten and a half miles and reckoned on getting there the following day since Freddie said there was only another twelve and a half miles to do. By starting early next day, and continuing on in the moonlight—luckily the full moon at this time of year shines nearly all night up here—we got within reach of our goal about 7 p.m. It was not easy. If we missed a flag by 100 yards or so we had to stop and all go in different directions to search for it. Flag 237 was down in the book as the end of the trail. After it seemed days of plodding through the darkness in the snow we found a flag and struck a match. Flag 236. Only half a mile to go. We could hardly get the dogs to go on again but at last we finished the half-mile. But where was the Union Jack? We searched in all directions expecting every minute to see it, and then warmth and dryness and *food*!! It was freezing over sixty degrees and the wind bit through our clothes as if we were naked. We went on a short distance further and searched again, but failed. At last we had to give it up. So wearily we pitched our tents and at length crawled into our stiff-frozen sleeping-bags. It was a bitter disappointment after what we had hoped. We slept little that night shivering with the cold of our frozen bags.

In the morning Freddie dashed out without wind-proofs to try and see the Station. Half an hour later he returned having seen nothing but having got both ears frost-bitten. He was foolish enough to warm them quickly in the tent. In a minute he was writhing in agony. [Wager wrote that he "almost wept and threw himself about the tent in the agony of ears and hands coming back."] It was the worst pain he had known, he said. As regards the disappearance of the Station, we could not make out what had happened. According to the book, the station ought to be at Flag 237 and that flag was close by. Wager went out to see what happened further on and came to 238 and then 239. We again inspected the traverse book. Then we found it. On a back page were scribbled more flags up to 262. This meant that we still had eleven miles to go. By the time we discovered this it was past noon. But we lashed up as quickly as we could, determined to try and make it that night if we possibly could and not spend another of misery like the last. The daylight soon went, the sun set about 2.30, but the good old moon came to our rescue so that we could travel on. The going was good and, although we had several anxious moments hunting for flags, Freddie made a very good course steering by the stars and at last about 6 p.m. we found a flag with a letter and a tin of Horlicks. This was written by D'Aeth on October 15th and it was a very cheering thing to get. We plodded on and eventually the sledge wheel showed we had done the distance. It was then freezing 80 degrees. Another night in our frozen bags was unthinkable. We all separated to do another moonlight hunt for the Station. I walked out across the snow until I lost sight of the sledges. Nothing. Would this be another trick of fate after another never-ending day? Must we again shiver all night in those ice-encrusted tents? I wandered back to the sledges feeling hopeless. As I got nearer to my sledge I saw the other two were back. Freddie shouted: "We have seen the Union Jack." I have never been so suddenly overcome with joy or been delivered in such a short moment from the depths of despair. In a few moments the low mound of snow with its tattered flag that is the place showed up in the moonlight. Stopping the sledges we advanced quickly inside the snow wall, reached the undersnow entrance and then yelled: "Evening Standard, Star and News!"

We burrowed down the hole, along the passage, and coming up into the tent found D'Aeth and Doc sitting there as warm and comfortable as could be, smoking their pipes. Being three weeks overdue, they were naturally jolly pleased to see us. We soon had our dogs out of their harnesses and were with them wolfing down the brew they had made for us, and giving them lots of news from the outside world. It was an epic evening after such a journey, but the joy of it was somewhat spoilt for me by intense pain in my fingers and toes from frost-bite. Freddie and I slept in one of the snow houses or igloos that open out of the tunnel leading to the main tent, which itself is covered by a snow house. It was cold, but breakfast the next morning with the others, a really late gentlemanly breakfast, was fine.

December 4th

WAGER — Still no time to describe the Ice Cap Station. Got up at 10 a.m. when the second meteorological readings are made. Had a large helping of porridge and tea. At twelve we turned out into the blizzard to collect some of the things that required sorting over or mending. Pottered about getting ready for the start which we hope will be tomorrow, but the wind is still high. This has prevented our patching the sledges or lashing our loads on as we should have liked to do.

I am again writing in the igloo with its fascinating beehive shape—yet made out of rectangular blocks— and the walls here and there sparkling from the crystal faces.

BINGHAM — Courtauld wants to stay alone, but I have given a very decided opinion against it.

COURTAULD — Doc and the others do not like my idea of staying here alone as it may be for three or four months, but short of abandoning the Station there is no alternative as there is only food [for one man] for that period.

CHAPMAN — We had a marvellous if somewhat premature Christmas dinner of special delicacies we had brought up from the Base for that purpose. The menu was as follows:

Ice Cap Christmas Dinner

Game soup
Sardines in Olive Oil
Ptarmigan
. Plum Pudding
Rum Sauce (very)
Angels on Sledges
Dessert (Dates and Raisins)
Mincemeat, Jam, Hot Grog, Tea (with milk)
Note—NO PEMMICAN

Though I cooked it, the dinner was better than any other dinner has ever been.

December 5th, Friday

WAGER — They apparently consider that there is too much wind, for we have not got up at six o'clock. I do not know the time but guess it to be 10 or 11 a.m. The others are not up and have closed the entrance to the tent where they are all sleeping to make it warmer. I have lighted a primus in my snow hut and may now have a moment to describe the Ice Cap Station.

As one arrives one sees the eight-foot snow wall which circles the tent and the snow houses making a courtyard. I have barely seen the outside because we arrived in the dark, and since then there has been the blizzard, one of the worst they have had so far in [from the coast] but nothing compared with some of ours, except the temperature has been very low. The central tent is about twelve feet in diameter, and cupola-shaped. An outside layer of snow hut has been built round it and no sound of the blizzard can generally be heard unless the primus is out, then there is a feeble sound coming through the ventilator. The hut has two raised divans made from empty boxes. In between, there is a skin on the floor and then a box for

the primus and lamp. These keep the hut pleasantly warm and at times the primus is turned out and the hut kept warm enough by the lamp alone. The entrance is by tunnel about five feet below the floor level, and in this pit the air is as cold as outside.

The tunnel is about twenty feet long and has two branches to snow huts which are built of snow blocks as described by Stefansson. The bluish light comes through the snow and especially along the joins be-

After a
blizzard

Moth aircraft before and after a storm

tween the blocks and gives a good and rather pleasant tho' cold light. I have been quite unsuccessful in warming my igloo with the primus, and I believe they are much colder than our tents—also a good deal bigger, being about 8 feet in diameter and $4\frac{1}{2}$ to 5 feet high.

D'Aeth and Doc have been here nine weeks. They got a certain amount of exercise throwing the snow over the wall out of the courtyard. They only went one walk, to leave a message for us four miles away. There is no point in walking. They have read all the books, written a good few letters, told each other all their stories, and smoked all their cigarettes, but they have tobacco. They do not look fit, and though they ate full sledging rations for the first few weeks have since been eating less because, I suppose, of their monotony. The Doc says that for about a fortnight, about the middle of their time, he used to get very out of breath and wake up in the night sweating and panting. Both have gradually been able to sleep less.

We on our side, who have spent five weeks getting here, have found the last part somewhat of a strain—tempers have been worse and disappointments more keen. Being cramped up in small tents has been less bearable, and the cold has sometimes almost made us weep. I hate getting off my stiff sealskin anorak [hooded smock] because it sticks and I suffer from a feeling of suffocation. Both Freddie and I found it a strain keeping a course and looking out for flags.

Courtauld seems quite cheerful about staying here for three months by himself. There is not enough food for me to stay too. We are leaving six full S.R. boxes [twelve weeks' full rations for one man] and a few odds and ends. When we arrived and heard there were two whole boxes left I again half expected to be staying. I don't think I should care for more than one month here by myself.

When we start back we hope to reach the Base in ten travelling days. We shall have for the four of us only two S.R. boxes (i.e. half-ration for a fortnight). Only two days full dog food and also about 30 lb. of spare man pemmican and 20 of margarine.

10.30 *p.m.*—Too windy to start even in the afternoon, and I think we are glad as we have been able to spend most of the day getting properly ready. Two sledges lashed with most attractively small loads. Poor old Bruno fed to the other dogs and mercifully they eat him. More drying done, but above all we are feeling better, at any rate I am, and I am looking forward to tomorrow especially as it promises to be a good day.

CHAPMAN — Gale still going strong. Thank God we got here before it started. Spent today discussing what is to be done. The Doctor and D'Aeth are dead against one man staying alone. They say they have experienced it and they know. However, Courtauld is determined to stay, and eventually we gave in. I must say it would be a thousand pities to abandon the Station now, since it has been established and maintained with so much trouble. Courtauld is very keen to stay, and judging by Watkins' experience amongst the Labrador trappers it is not so bad as people make out.

CHAPTER VIII

Wegener's Eismitte

MAINTAINING a weather station on the middle line of the Ice Cap was proving even more difficult than had been expected. The problem for the leader on the spot was to balance risk of life against the value of continuing the scientific programme—the job they were there for. No more supplies could be brought up until that unknown date when the winter would end. What was the right thing to do—run for the coast all together or risk life for the sake of a meteorological record?

Much the same problem was being faced by Professor Alfred Wegener's German Expedition, three hundred miles further north. While Chapman's party was waiting for an opportunity to start back towards the Base, I will describe briefly the parallel adventure on the Ice Cap.

With his main party, Wegener had planned to approach the Ice Cap from the west. The west coast of Greenland is navigable while the east is still ice-bound, so he was able to begin work on land in June, two months earlier than we were.

The main Base was established on the western fringe of the Ice Cap, about latitude 71 degrees, and at once there began the transportation of stores for the setting up of a central station—Eismitte, as it was called.

PORTRAIT OF AN ICE CAP

Since Greenland is a good deal wider in latitude
71 degrees than in latitude 66 degrees, where we were,
the position of Wegener's Eismitte was about a hundred miles further from the coast than was our Ice Cap
Station. Also, for his wider scientific programme, he
required a greater weight of instruments. For trans-
port he had decided to depend not only on dogs but on
three forms of assistance of which we kept ourselves
independent—Eskimos, motor sledges, and Iceland
ponies for carrying on the coastal fringe.

On July 15th a start was made from the western
edge of the Ice Cap with three and a half tons of food
and equipment loaded onto twelve dog sledges. Three
of the party were Europeans—Dr. Georgi, Dr. Loewe
and Dr. Weiken—and the rest were Eskimos. From
the first the Eskimos were half-hearted. In spite of
their lifelong sledging experience they had never done
more than skirt the fringe of the Ice Cap when
travelling from one fjord to another. Whether or not
they were still affected by superstitious fears of the
evil spirits of the Ice Cap, they had, in their ordinary
lives, a sound reason for avoiding it. There was no
food there. Now the Europeans were giving them
their daily food, certain clothing and four kroner a day.
Four shillings a day was more than they could earn
on the coast. But to travel so far from the sea they
knew, climbing this endless, lifeless mountain which
became colder and colder and where even the dogs
grew listless and dispirited—they looked over their
shoulders.

Various concessions were made to encourage them.

Georgi dumped some of his precious equipment to lighten the loads, and attempts were made to explain the purpose of the journey. But when on July 22nd they reached the half-way point—125 miles—all the Eskimos said that they were going home.

This would have meant the failure of the whole Ice Cap plan. It was an anxious moment—far more than a moment, for the argument went on for hours. But at last four Eskimos agreed to continue with Georgi and Weiken while the remainder returned with Loewe to the friendly coast.

Georgi's party reached the position chosen for Eismitte on July 30th. Two days later Weiken and the Eskimos turned for home while Georgi remained in charge of the Station.

He was there alone until August 18th, when Loewe and five Eskimos arrived with an effective load of about one ton. They spent a night with him and then again left him alone, absorbed in his meteorological balloons and other instruments.

After another twenty-five days Dr. Sorge, Dr. Wölcken, Jülg and seven Eskimos arrived with a ton and a half of provisions, paraffin and equipment. Sorge was to be Georgi's companion for the winter. Checking over their stores they decided that unless the motor sledges arrived they would still lack some essential items. By digging a cave and pitching their tent in it, they could do without the wooden hut which had been intended. But they felt that they must have more paraffin. Also, Georgi needed wire for his meteorological kite and Sorge explosives for his echo soundings. They sent back a letter to Wegener saying that unless they received these things by October 20th they would walk out to the coast. They stated this merely as information to their leader. There seemed no doubt that the stores could be brought in, either by the motor sledges, which by now were on the Ice Cap and which were capable of covering the 250 miles in two days, or else by another dog-sledge party. None the less, this letter was one of the factors which affected the sequence of events.

Another was the fate of the motor sledges. The returning dog-sledge party, Wölken, Jülg and the seven Eskimos, met the two propeller-driven sledges at the 125-mile depot on September 17th. They drove on westward next morning before the motors had been started up.

Meanwhile Wegener, although of course still uninformed of these events, had decided that one more dog-sledge party must go in to make Eismitte secure for the winter. It was to be a very large party, no less than fifteen sledges. This meant hiring at least twelve Eskimos and over a hundred and fifty dogs. Partly to encourage the Eskimos and partly that he should be on hand for any decision that had to be made, he decided to lead the party himself.

Most of the loads were dragged up over the rough coastal ice by Iceland ponies. Ten miles inland the dog sledges were loaded, and the big convoy set off eastward.

They had covered scarcely two miles when they met Wölcken, Jülg and their seven Eskimos returning from

Eismitte. These handed Georgi's and Sorge's letter to Wegener. Since it was already September 21st it would be extremely difficult for Wegener to reach Eismitte by October 20th. But it seemed likely that this urgency no longer existed, for Wölcken and Jülg said they had met the motor sledges in running order at the half-way depot four days ago. The probability was that they had already stocked Eismitte with paraffin and the winter hut.

Wegener delayed one day longer to collect the items of equipment which Georgi and Sorge had asked for. Then he continued his journey towards Eismitte. But about thirty miles inland he had another meeting— with the motor-sledge party.

Crowded together in a little tent they told their story. When Wölcken and Jülg had left them after their encounter at the half-way depot, the morning had been misty. It was all right for dogs, but in motor sledges it was more difficult to follow the line of flags. They could not risk losing the way and wasting precious fuel. Therefore they decided to wait for better weather before beginning their one-day run to Eismitte, 125 miles away.

Instead of getting better weather they became snowed in. When they had dug out the sledges the engines were very slow to start. When at last they started they would not pull the heavy loads. At last the mechanics decided to return to the coast.

Wegener had put great faith in the propeller sledges, but he listened to this sad story without comment, quietly smoking his pipe. He was a man of forty-nine years and much experience. He was not only a professor of geophysics and meteorology but a fine leader of men. He accepted what had happened without apparent surprise. But this did not weaken his determination that Eismitte should be maintained throughout the winter. Therefore he must get there with the dog sledges by October 20th.

It was an ill-starred journey. The weather was warm but the snow was soft and deep. The big Eskimo dog teams floundered and got in each other's way, yet their drivers ignored each other's troubles since that is the native etiquette. And on September 28th there was a major crisis.

Before the morning start the Eskimos crawled one by one into the tent which Wegener and Loewe shared. They sat there packed together, smoking their pipes and looking at the floor. They said nothing—they were like sullen children.

At last it came out. Although it was still warm, the cold was sure to come and they had not enough clothing to face it. The loads were too heavy. They wanted to go home.

For hours the argument went on, slow, awkward, complicated by the lack of all but a few words of common language, complicated still more by the Eskimos' inability to understand an abstract idea like scientific study.

At last four men agreed to go on at an increased rate of pay while the rest went back to the coast. With these four Wegener and Loewe struggled through deep warm snow towards Eismitte. Time was vital, for at this season the weather could only deteriorate. But they could not travel fast. And they were never certain of the Eskimos on whom they were dependent. Of necessity, the load for Eismitte had already been very severely cut. They could not afford more trouble and delay.

The uneasy partnership lasted until October 5th, when Detlev, the old hunter who acted as spokesman, said that he and the other three now definitely wanted to go home. So again the slow arguments began. They continued for two precious days on and off. Finally Detlev and two others went back, while the last Eskimo, Rasmus, expressed himself as ready to go on with Wegener and Loewe for the whole distance.

Rasmus was a good man. He was only twenty-two years old and had no doubt been influenced by the old hunters. Once he had made up his mind and had parted with his fellow Eskimos he could not have been more loyal nor worked harder. He went in front, breaking the trail through the deep powder snow and, with his wonderfully quick eyes, picking up the flags in the dusk through which they travelled.

But their difficulties were still very far from being over. Try as they would they could not average as much as ten miles a day. As they struggled slowly on, the load intended for Eismitte was gradually consumed or dumped. All the equipment for the Station had to be left behind. And soon it became evident that they could not hope to arrive before October 20th. Often they wondered if it were possible to arrive at all. By now they could be of little or no help to Georgi and Sorge. But if they turned back, and if Georgi and Sorge did not arrive on the coast, the uncertainty over the two men's fate would grow intolerable during the winter. That was Wegener's opinion. Besides, he was determined that Eismitte should not be abandoned if he could at almost any risk prevent it.

On every journey there comes a point after which it is more difficult to turn back than to go on. In this case it was calculated to be the 143-mile mark. They went beyond this point. On October 20th they had reached the 181-mile mark. Thereafter they expected to meet Georgi and Sorge, but they did not. By now the man food and fuel were dangerously low and the dogs were starving. The only chance was to press on as quickly as possible and share the small supplies at Eismitte. They had become dependent on the Station which they had set out to restock.

The last part of the journey was terribly hard. The temperature had so far remained comparatively high. But now when men and dogs were at their weakest it suddenly dropped to the region of forty or fifty degrees below zero. By October 30th the last of the paraffin was finished. Wegener, Loewe and Rasmus heated up a small meal over their emergency solid fuel and covered the final miles to Eismitte.

The ice cave seemed wonderfully warm—there were only ten degrees of frost as opposed to ninety or more outside. And the chamber itself, hewn out and furnished with such intricate and ingenious care by the two scientists, was as comfortable as a modern home. Georgi and Sorge were still there. They had

decided they could last out the winter after all. But
the three newcomers could not remain for they had
arrived virtually without food and fuel. Loewe was
compelled to stay. Both his feet were badly frost-
bitten, and shortly afterwards he had all his toes
amputated by Georgi, with a pocket-knife and without
an anaesthetic. But Wegener decided to start back with
Rasmus after only two nights' rest. He was in high
spirits, rubbing his hands with pleasure at having
reached Eismitte and found it not only secure but so
comfortable. He and Rasmus were both in good
physical condition and the Eismitte stores were able to
provide them with 300 lb. of provisions and a can of
paraffin.

On November 1st Professor Wegener celebrated his
fiftieth birthday. Then he and Rasmus set off for the
coast, their seventeen thin dogs harnessed to two
lightly loaded sledges.

The three men who remained at Eismitte could hear
nothing until April. Wegener would have the wind
behind him and there were depots of food upon the
way. When December came they hoped that he had
reached the coast.

From the coastal Base a relief party set out in
November. They managed to travel about fifty miles
eastward and left a depot of food. Each night they lit
flares which must have been visible for a long distance.
Before starting, Wegener had given December 1st as
the latest date for his return. The relief party remained
upon the Ice Cap until December 7th. As a matter of
interest, this was the day after Chapman, Wager,

Bingham and D'Aeth began their return journey, having left Courtauld at the Ice Cap Station.

It is convenient to anticipate here what was discovered about Wegener's last journey. Not until April 21st of the following year was it found possible to start a relief journey to Eismitte. Then a dog-sledge party set out. They were followed by a motor-sledge party, with Rasmus' brother as a passenger, and the two parties reached Eismitte almost simultaneously. As soon as they met the three men who had wintered there they all realised without words what must have happened.

At once a search was started for the bodies. Near the 158-mile mark, less than half-way to the coast, Wegener's sledge was found. From there he and Rasmus must have gone on with one sledge between them, presumably because the mortality among their seventeen dogs had been heavy. By the 118-mile mark, 132 miles from Eismitte, Wegener's skis were found stuck upright in the snow.

The search party dug down through the winter-fallen snow and two and a half feet below the surface of last November. There they found Wegener. He had been sewn into two sleeping-bag covers and was lying on his sleeping-bag and a reindeer skin. His clothing had been carefully brushed clean of snow, just as one used to do before coming into a tent. Everything was in perfect order. He was wearing blue cloth trousers with dog-skin trousers over them, a shirt, blue waist-coat, blue ski-ing tunic, a thick sweater, helmet and peaked cap. His fur boots—which need daily attention on a journey—were in excellent condition.

His face seemed younger than when they had seen it last. His eyes were open and his expression was absolutely peaceful, almost smiling. He was rather pale though, and there were small frost-bites on his cheeks, such as often showed in the evening during winter travel. He must have come into the tent as usual, lain down and died. Rasmus had cared for him, had taken on his diary and other personal effects.

Travelling westward the search-party found near the 105-mile mark signs that Rasmus had camped there for several days. There was a hatchet which he had carried and the remains of several meals. Between there and the coast, none of the food depots had been touched. Rasmus was never found.

From the date of his start from Eismitte and the distance that he covered it seems probable that Wegener died about November 20th, and Rasmus not long after. Thus when Courtauld was left alone on December 6th, the Ice Cap had already claimed two lives. Wegener had been buried by Rasmus. Rasmus must also have been buried, by the snow. He was lying as he still must lie, perfectly preserved by the thing which had killed him. If someone found him now or in a hundred years' time I suppose they would be able to recognise even the expression of his face.

.   .   .   .   .

Picturing yourself in the situation of a man who remains alone on the Ice Cap for the winter, the first thing you probably think about is the loneliness, for very few people have been more than one day entirely by themselves. Certainly no place can be lonelier than the Ice Cap. And if I have conveyed anything of its character you will understand that it is easy to be frightened by it. It threatens none of the personal vindictiveness you might fear among wild animals or head-hunters in a jungle. There are virtually none of the dangers of what we call civilised life. For instance you would not even catch a cold. It is unlikely that you would break a leg. The Ice Cap is aloof and indifferent—and vast. It is its vast indifference which is so frightening. Anywhere else when you are tired you can sit down and rest. You cannot do that on the Ice Cap in the winter-time, or not for long. If you drop a glove your hand is frozen in a moment. Suffering some trivial accident it would not take long for your whole body to go numb. And, worst of all, cold stultifies the brain like a drug.

The weather instruments were only a few yards from the exit of the tunnel. But in a thick blizzard it would have been quite easy to lose the sense of direction. Then—a few paces in the wrong line, a fit of panic and a brain that would not work. . . . The driving snow would soon cover you when you fell.

There is another aspect of being alone—the physical strain. From Riley's diary and still more from Bingham's it has been made evident how much digging they had to do to keep the tunnel clear, to keep themselves from being buried. This had been done by two men. Now one must do it all. He must go out for every one of the six observations every day. He must do all the cooking, all the mending, all the household chores without relief. Quite apart from the mental loneliness, a big physical strain was involved in one man maintaining the Station.

CHAPTER IX

A Winter Alone

December 6th, Saturday

COURTAULD — Today broke fine so it was time for them to go. I got up at 3.30 and cooked their breakfast. By ten they were ready. I took a photo and then with a "Damma, damma, damma" they were away down the trail. Although there was a feeble sun, it was bitterly cold and I did not watch them long. Coming out again an hour later I could just see them as a speck in the distance. Now I am quite alone. Not a dog or even a mosquito for company. However it is very comfortable, or will be when I have cleared up the mess a bit. The great problem at the moment is to get my things dry. My sleeping-bag is full of ice and all my clothes except what I have got on are the same. Still my pipe tastes just as ever and the igloo is warm, so really there is nothing to complain of unless it be the curse of having to go out every three hours into the cold wind to observe the weather.

December 7th, Sunday—Fine and cold (56 degrees below). Up at 7 a.m. for the first observation. Breakfast about 10.30. Lunch 2.30. Supper 7.30. With a certain amount of tidying up in between. Left little finger painful and swollen, also both big toes.

December 8th, Monday—Cold clear day again. Sun did not rise and I suppose will not until the middle of

A WINTER ALONE

SECTION

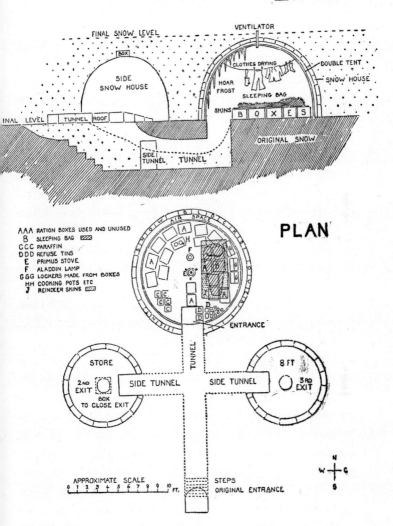

ORIGINAL SNOW
DRIFT SNOW

FINAL SNOW LEVEL
VENTILATOR
BOX
SIDE SNOW HOUSE
CLOTHES DRYING
DOUBLE TENT
SNOW HOUSE
HOAR FROST
SLEEPING BAG
SKINS
FINAL LEVEL
TUNNEL ROOF
B O X E S
SIDE TUNNEL
TUNNEL
ORIGINAL SNOW

PLAN

AAA RATION BOXES USED AND UNUSED
B SLEEPING BAG
CCC PARAFFIN
DDD REFUSE TINS
E PRIMUS STOVE
F ALADDIN LAMP
GGG LOCKERS MADE FROM BOXES
HH COOKING POTS ETC
J REINDEER SKINS

SNOW BLOCKS AIR SPACE

ENTRANCE

STORE
2ND EXIT
BOX TO CLOSE EXIT
SIDE TUNNEL
TUNNEL
SIDE TUNNEL
8 FT
3RD EXIT

APPROXIMATE SCALE
0 1 2 3 4 5 6 7 8 9 10 FT.

STEPS
ORIGINAL ENTRANCE

N
W   E
S

next month. Got on with drying clothes in intervals between met. observations which happen at 7, 10, 1, 4, 7 and 10.

December 9th, Tuesday—Nothing of note today except that I changed my underclothes as I had had itching for the last night or two. Found a good many bugs, much to my disgust, so put my clothes out in the snow in the pious hope that the cold will kill them. This is what comes of lending one's sleeping-bag to Eskimos.

December 10th, Wednesday—Did some tidying up. Lamp lit first time today instead of taking four hours as it did yesterday. No more signs of bugs.

December 11th, Thursday—Toes hurting, also fingers. Took an observation of Aldebaran to find how much the clock has gone wrong in the last three months. Reading *Forsyte Saga*, Vol. II—V.G. Even better than Vol. I. Opened pea-flour and marge today. Found jam made out of cocoa V.G., much better than drinking it, and agree in this respect with G.K.C. Filled paraffin cans (4 gallons).

December 12th, Friday—Windy day with drifting snow. House went down to 35 degrees but primus put it to 60 degrees again. Stopped up ventilation hole to try and keep in heat at night. Entrance to tunnel blocked up when I went out for 10 p.m. obs. Had to dig my way out. This weather won't help the others getting back. Filled pemmican bag, 1½ lb.

December 13th, Saturday—Strong N.W. wind blowing snow so that one could hardly see to get out to the instruments. A blizzard in fact. Entrance to tunnel completely stopped up and had to dig myself out for every observation. Played a game of chess this evening and then bandaged toes. Both seem quite dead but are gooing.

December 14*th*, *Sunday*—Dug out the entrance this morning, but the wind shifted to S.E. and filled it up again. V. warm, temperature went up to plus 5 degrees. Found I am only smoking 1·7 oz. a week. Tobacco should last at this rate seventeen weeks. Reading *Black Arrow*, *Friendly Arctic*, Isaak. All V.G. What I shall do when I have finished all the books God knows. Made out a list for a chap's dinner when I get home.

December 15*th*, *Monday*—Amazingly warm day, plus 7 degrees. Change of wind has completely drifted up the courtyard as well as the entrance to the house so now one has to wade knee-deep in snow, after fighting one's way out of the tunnel, and then climb over a six-foot drift to get outside the walls. A further wade, tripping over ridges and falling into invisible holes in the diffused light brings one to the instruments. Filled plasmon bag, $\frac{1}{2}$ lb.

December 16*th*, *Tuesday*—Still this warm wind blowing stronger than ever. Had a job to get out of house this morning. Found I was digging up into a vast snow drift, so had to make a hole vertically upwards, and after some time burrowing managed to scramble out. Got lost getting to the instruments at seven o'clock for the drift was too thick. Tonight unbandaged toes. Unpleasant sight. Left toe-nail came off. Other will soon, I expect.

December 17*th, Wednesday*—A calmer day. Spent a long time digging out the tunnel. Got it fairly clear by dark. Quite a warm pleasant night, little wind and only 36 degrees of frost. Filled up pea-flour and pemmican. Seven hours a day of primus with lamp on all day just fail to last two gallons of paraffin a week, so am trying the arse warmer for a week and only use the primus for cooking.

December 19*th, Friday*—All today and yesterday N.W. gale blew, which completely snowed up the entrance to tunnel again. Today had to dig self out every three hours.

December 20*th, Saturday*—Still blowing. Had great difficulty in getting out of tunnel. Full of snow. Quieter a bit in the evening with fine aurora. Although 70 degrees of frost it was quite pleasant to stand outside and look at it.

December 21*st, Sunday*—A peaceful day at last. Went out to do some digging about noon and saw the old sun, or half of it, for the first time for a fortnight. Aurora wonderful tonight, like purple smoke wreaths twisting and writhing all over the sky. At ten o'clock it was completely still. The silence was almost terrible. Nothing to hear but one's heart beating and the blood ticking in one's veins.

Other toe-nail came off tonight. Looks very nasty, all soft, dead and gooing.

December 24*th, Wednesday*—Christmas Eve. How wonderful it would be at home or Cod. This time last year was such a marvellous Xmas. The last three days here have been quiet and pleasant enough. Spent as much time outside as daylight and toes would allow, digging away the results of the gales.

Thank God the shortest day is now past. Found that two of the paraffin tins have been leaking so I am down to four gallons. This means I shall have to economise with heating. I wonder what they are doing at home. B. I suppose in Switz. I wonder if she has taken W. with her. I really do not miss the good things of Xmas very much. Though I would rather like a bit of fresh meat and a mince pie, and even more a bit of plum pudd. If only I had reckoned on spending Christmas here I could have brought some good things from W.'s F. and M. boxes, but it seems that on this show no prearranged plan ever gets fulfilled. Found a further edition of bugs in my clothes tonight so changed and applied a liberal quantity of Keatings.

December 25th, Thursday, Christmas—How jolly if I was at home or even at the Base. I suppose they will be having a blind and finishing the last of the alc. However I have not done so badly. Excellent porridge for breakfast and a tin of shrimp paste; peas for dinner and a supper of rice, honey (made from sugar and marge) and toffee (home-made) and chocolate. Pipe (W.'s) going V.G. Books good: Jane Austen and *Great Sea Stories*, and nothing to disturb the peace except the wind whistling up to an increasing gale, and the house, which is making rather frightening cracks and thumps. Hope it isn't going to fall in. If only I could put the clock on to next Christmas. How marvellous it will be to get back next summer. If plans go according to their appointed destinies—which they probably won't—I think I should like a small house in Suffolk between twenty and sixty miles from H. Should be near for trains and near the sea, preferably Pin Mill. No land except a garden and fewest possible servants. No waiting at table. If any money would rather spend it on a boat than a house. Something like *Colona* would be V.G. though possibly a little small for long passages. A Brixham trawler would be almost ideal but would probably cost a lot to make habitable. It would be better to keep her at Falmouth or somewhere on the South coast than on the East coast from which one can get nowhere without a long and tedious passage.

December 27th, Saturday—North-east wind has drifted up the whole place again. Did a certain amount of digging today and yesterday, but toes hurt too much to stay out more than a few minutes at a time. It is now just three weeks since the others left. Had an awful fright early this morning. Just getting to sleep again after 7 a.m. obs. when there was a soft rumbling close to my head which increased and ended in a dull crash. It flashed across my mind as it began that the weight of snow was too much and the whole house was going to come in on me. However nothing happened so I concluded that the tunnel had fallen in and that I should have a job to get out as the spade would be buried. However that was not so and I think that some of the blocks in the wall of the house have given way and fallen in but it is impossible to find out until a lot of snow has been removed from the top. Hope nothing further happens tonight.

I wonder when and how we shall get home.

Whether we shall land in London, Copenhagen, Harwich or where. If Harwich I shall wire for W. [his name for the lady he married] to meet me. I hope it is. If London or Aberdeen she could meet me in L. but not so easily. Have been studying the map of Scotland (having a Bart.'s pocket atlas, thank God) and it is quite obvious I must do another cruise with W. on the west coast. One might charter *Colona*. *Cariad* is a good ship though she is hardly comfortable enough and too heavy on her gear; also she won't go to windward in a sea.

December 31*st* (11.30 *p.m.*)—New Year's Eve. It is certainly quiet. The last few days have been fine and cool with some magnificent aurorae. Expecting to see the sun again any day now. Opened new ration box yesterday. Started biscuits, plasmon and chocolate. Filled pea-flour today. Toes have been hurting considerably lately so bathed and bandaged them. Did a bit of spring cleaning for the New Year. Discovering lots of useful and amusing information in Whitaker. Shall make a list of books lately published therefrom. N.Y. Resolutions:

(1) Mend moccasins and sleeping-bag.

(2) Get home and ask W. to marry me.

(3) Find (*a*) a house (Suffolk, Sussex or Dorset); (*b*) a boat; (*c*) a job. ((*a*) and (*b*) rather depend on condition of financial affairs when I get home.)

(4) Give up exploring.

(5) Collect a library and study: (*a*) English literature and poetry; (*b*) Music; (*c*) Polar exploration with a view possibly to try to write a book about it.

PORTRAIT OF AN ICE CAP

Wish I could send a wireless to W. Wonder how they are doing at the Base—finishing up the last of the good eats and drinks I suppose.

January 1st—A fine day. Had full ration of porridge for breakfast, rice-pudding for lunch and whole slab of chocolate. Hope weather keeps like this. With toes and fingers in present condition it is no fun digging oneself out every three hours and digging snow off the house as one has to do whenever it blows. These fine moonlight nights are quite jolly to wander about in so long as one doesn't stay out too long. Took an observation of Mars tonight to check the time. It is curious that it doesn't get any colder. The mean temperature for December is higher than November and now it has been about minus 30 degrees or minus 35 degrees for several days with north wind instead of descending as it did last month to minus 50 degrees or minus 55 degrees. Started pemmican, paraffin and porridge today. Only have fourteen gallons of paraffin left.

LIST OF BOOKS WORTH READING TAKEN FROM ICE CAP LIBRARY, JANUARY 1ST

Purchas His Pilgrimes.
Martin Chuzzlewit, Dickens.
A Tarpaulin Muster, Masefield.
The Brassbounder, Bone.
The Ghost Ship and Other Tales, Middleton (Benn).
Two Years Before the Mast, Dana.
The Golden Key, Van Dyke (Scribner).

120

A WINTER ALONE

Under Sail, Riesenburg (Cape).
Fenceless Meadows, Adams (Hutchinson).
Great Waters, Hutchinson.
Almanach des Gourmands, M. Florence.
Life of C. M. Doughty, Hogarth.
Peter the Great, Graham.
My Brother Jonathan, Young.
Joseph and his Brethren, Freeman.
Portrait in a Mirror, Morgan.
The Legion of the Damned, Doty.
Cambridge History of Empire, Vols. I-IV.
The Star Spangled Manner, Nichols.
The Art of Forgetting, Shepard.
Essays and Fantasies, Lucas.
The Aftermath, Churchill.
The Nature of the Physical World, Eddington.
The Universe Around Us, Jeans.
The Compleat Angler, Walton.
Great Poems of the English Language, Harrap.
The Red Rover, Fenimore Cooper.

January 4th, Sunday—A frightful day. There was a gale blowing when I woke up this morning and of course the tunnel was snowed up. Managed to dig self out and came back with clothes full of snow which got over everything. One piece dropped inside the lamp and broke the mantle. Dug out again at eleven o'clock, 1 and 2.30. Each time the entrance was blocked right up and snow drifting in about as fast as I could dig. By this time (2.30) the back of the tunnel was so full of snow caused by digging out the entrance that I could scarcely wriggle up it. At 2 the drift at the entrance was deeper than my height and I had some difficulty in getting out even when I had dug away the snow. At 3.30 I found I could no longer get the snow back from the entrance. The tunnel was too full already and the wind was still increasing. It is blowing a full gale blizzard, and outside one can hardly see one's spade, and one's face gets covered up directly. So, as I cannot get out, I shall have to stay in and the met. will have to go hang till the wind drops. Then I shall have to find some way of getting out. Hope the air keeps breathable and that the roof doesn't collapse. If (*a*) doesn't or (*b*) does my end should be peaceful enough, and I have four slabs of chocolate to eat during it. Anyhow it won't be attended by the fuss and frills one's pegging out at home would.

January 5th, Monday—Came to the conclusion this morning that it was impossible to dig out the tunnel, so dug out the entrance of the starboard snow house and cut a hole in the roof. Luckily it did not fall in and so I was able to get out. THANK GOD.

The gale which rose again this morning calmed down by evening and so all is once more peaceful.

January 6th, Tuesday—It is just a month now since the others left. Had a quiet day today. The hole of the roof of the snow house proves quite a convenient exit.

Had a jump this evening. As I was in a sort of doze I heard W. call me twice "Aug, Aug." The time was about 11 p.m. G.M.T.

The obvious idea for a west coast cruise would be

to sail up the east coast and through the Forth-Clyde Canal. Pick her up on the Clyde and then through the Kyles of Bute and Crinan Canal to Oban. Thence to all the good places: Loch Linnhe, Aline, Torridon, Cairnbarn, etc. One might come back through the Caledonian or down the Irish Sea or down east coast. Irish Sea would be the pleasantest in some ways as one could call at Kingstown and Falmouth, but it could be long.

January 7th, Wednesday—Filled up pemmican bag.

January 12th, Monday—Nothing much happened the last few days. Rather vile weather except for Saturday when the sun came up for the first time since December 21st. Started paraffin today and plasmon yesterday. Weather warm and quiet at present but showing signs of easterly gale.

January 14th, Wednesday—Blew hard from west this morning, now still as death and dark as pitch. Barometer dropping like a stone. Suppose something pretty unpleasant is about to happen. Reading *Guy Mannering* (Scott), V.V.G. Descriptions of food make one writhe, worse than *Forsyte Saga*. But I like reading about it. The Potage à la Meg Merrilees sounds marvellous.

January 15th, Thursday—Ideas of electrical met. instruments.

January 16th, Friday—Felt rather faint yesterday at 4 p.m. probably as a consequence of turning on the blasted arse warmer. Thought I should not be able to get back into house. However all was well although heart beating very fast. Gave myself a rest for six hours so missed 7 p.m. obs. Cold wind and drift today, temp. minus 46 degrees. House showing signs of collapsing. Wish I could get snow dug off the roof. Would have done so yesterday if I had not felt so bad. Cannot stay out more than a few minutes as feet freeze up so quickly. Finished *Guy Mannering*. Jolly good book.

January 21st, Wednesday—Just finished *Jane Eyre*. It's a great book, one of the best I have ever read. How she can have written it in those early Victorian days is past imagination. The sun came up yesterday and today. It is grand to see it casting its rose-pink light along the snow, making dark shadows and bright places so that one's eyes blink.

January 23rd, Friday—Only ten gallons of paraffin left now. Weather cold and fine with north wind. Quite pleasant in the middle of the day but too cold to stay out long without elaborate dressing up.

January 28th, Wednesday—Finished *Wuthering Heights*. Read it before in Greenland 1926. It is a fine book but I don't like it so much as *J.E.* although, I suppose, a greater work. The plot seems too unreal, the tone too dreary and the characters too monstrous. Now reading Pepys and *Vanity Fair*. The latter, having read it before, seems excellent. A full gale is blowing at present and nearly succeeded, the night before last, in blocking up the bolt-hole in the snow house which is my only exit nowadays. Other misfortunes have been the parangara [destruction] of the barometer and the maximum thermometer, both through my carelessness. The former I dropped a cooking-pot on and the latter broke while cleaning the snow off it. Although, previous to this blizzard, there had been several days of bright fine weather, but very cold, there has been no sign of the aeroplane. I very much doubt if it will come now. Probably it cannot take off, so I suppose I shall have to wait a few more months until someone can sledge here.

February 1st, Sunday—After the south-east gale had finished—this gale blew so hard that I had to walk or rather stagger backwards to get to the observations —it started again from north-west. In the meantime the paraffin has nearly run out in the house, and I cannot dig the other tin out while these gales are blowing. Tried digging but did not locate it. Of course the hole fills up directly one stops digging. The fact is I am not sure of its exact position now that everything is drifted up with snow. Changed clothes tonight for the original inhabited ones, but the inmates have been done down by leaving them out in the cold. Just finished *Vanity Fair*. Liked it well. There is something very satisfying in reading perfect English whatever the story and have now started de Quincey's *Opium Eater* which seems very long-winded and pedantic, but again it is well worth reading for its style.

I wonder when, if ever, I shall get away from here. Not that I am bored, but I notice that my legs are getting very thin, partly from want of exercise and partly from lack of fresh food I suppose. If I have to sledge back it will be pretty rotten unless the going is good enough to ride. These gales are nerve-racking things. I am daily expecting the house to fall in, for both the side snow houses have partly done so. I wish there could be some decent weather. Whenever the sun is out and it is clear it is about 50 degrees below zero, and the rest of the time it blows blizzards so that one can see or do nothing on account of the drift.

February 3rd, Tuesday—Got the paraffin out after a lot of digging yesterday. Luckily I had on W.'s mittens, otherwise my hands would have been frozen. It was almost six feet deep. Just finished Pepys (Braybrook edition). Wish it was continued further.

February 6th, Friday—Now been alone here just two months. Finished de Quincey's *Opium Eater*. Do not care for it. Too pedantic although English is perfect. Also it is plagued with footnotes. Now reading Dorothy Osborne's letters. Good. Weather cold with north-west wind.

February 8th, Sunday—Daddy's birthday. Celebrated with boiled rice for lunch and made some toffee. Fine and sunny in the middle of day but cold north wind (minus 40 degrees to minus 45 degrees). Reading *Tess of the d'Urbs* again, V.G. especially the first part.

February 14th, Saturday—Have now been ten weeks alone. Weather this week has been damnable. First of all too cold to do any digging (90 degrees of frost) so that I am running short of rations because the others are buried about ten feet under snow. Then I left the opening of the snow-house roof unstopped one night and it came on to blow from the south-east and filled it up completely. With great difficulty I got it a bit clear and stopped it coming in from that direction,

when last night it went back to the north-west and
filled it up again. Now impossible to get out without
letting all the snow down into the tunnel, which is so
small now that I can only just wriggle through it.
Only one more day's food after today. Still blowing.

February 17*th, Tuesday*—On Sunday morning found
the snow house completely filled up and could not
get out till ten o'clock. Then having blown a south-
east gale all night, it turned round and started again
from the north-west. Very cold, minus 50 degrees.
However this did not develop so strongly as before,
and Monday was a fairly decent day. Tried to dig out
the ration boxes but fingers and toes froze up before I
could get down to them. It then came on to blow from
the south-east and of course filled up the hole. I
stopped the entrance up as well as I could, but directly
I had got back into bed it started blowing harder than
ever. Could not get out this morning till ten o'clock
by which time it was calm. As the outside boxes
seemed unobtainable and as I had run out of all the
palatable rations I started work on the one buried in
the snow house. It was slow work digging away the
concrete snow and filling it into biscuit tins to empty
outside. After two hours I got at it and burst it open
with the screw-driver. As a last blow found it was one
of the ones that had been pilfered of chocolate. However, thank God, I have got something decent to eat
out of it. Came on to blow again this evening from the
west, barometer crashing. Hope to goodness the entrance stopping doesn't come in again or I shall be
snowed up for good. In two hours it nearly filled the

snow house. Read *Master of Ballantrae*, V.G. Hope the chaps have not set out from the Base yet. This weather is impossible for sledging. As far as I can see six months at least of the expedition will be a complete waste of time. All the proposed long sledge journeys will go to pot.

February 19*th, Thursday*—Gale continued all yesterday and most of today. A terrifying thing happened at 5.30 this evening. I was reading in here as usual when I heard a rushing sound seeming to come from behind and increasing in a second to a roar like an avalanche. It ended suddenly with a crash like thunder. I thought at first I was going to be overwhelmed in some sort of snow whirlwind. Then as nothing happened I thought one of the snow houses had fallen in and I should be imprisoned, but there seemed too big a noise for that. On getting outside at seven o'clock everything appeared as before, nothing having collapsed. What it was I cannot think unless some chasm forming in the ice underneath. It sounded most like thousands of tons of snow falling in an avalanche.

· · · · ·

February 25*th, Wednesday*

SCOTT — On February 25th, the first opportunity, Cozens and I flew in from the Base hoping to find the Ice Cap Station and to drop food. We saw no sign of the Station or even of the flags which had marked the route.

· · · · ·

A WINTER ALONE

COURTAULD — At last the gales have died down and given way to cold clear weather though the northwest wind still blows. The temperature has been down to minus 60 degrees. Am getting thoroughly fed up with going out to the observations every three hours and getting all outer clothes covered with snow by having to wriggle through the tunnel. Am down to the last four gallons of paraffin now. If the others don't turn up in three or four weeks, I shall be reduced to cold and darkness. If ever I get back to the Base nothing will induce me to go on the Ice Cap again. When the others will come God knows. These gales will have made sledging impossible and have raised drifts like young hills even here. What the going is like further out Heaven knows. Judging by when we arrived, when the going here was good, I should think it's absolutely impossible.

CHAPTER X

The First Relief Attempt

O N March 1st Quintin Riley and I made our first attempt to sledge in to relieve Courtauld at the Ice Cap Station. We had "a tearful farewell" from the Eskimos, who seemed to take it for granted that we would never return.

We were back again next day, with a sledge broken in half by the big hard drifts. And we made a second false start before we got away finally—with Martin Lindsay making the party up to three—on March 9th.

It was early in the season for travelling on the Ice Cap. Winter was still full of strength. Even at the Base the gales were extremely powerful. They kept blowing down the wireless masts, trundling the stores about or burying them, and making the hut shiver and jump under the wire ropes which held it to the rocks. Gino had apologetically told me that he would not have sent us out so soon if the aeroplane had been able to drop food to Courtauld, or even to see him and the Station. But after the one unsuccessful flight which I had made with Cozens both aeroplanes had been out of commission, badly damaged by the storms. There could be no certainty as to when they would be repaired or that they could find the Station when they were. So we began our sledge journey as soon as it seemed practicable.

I must explain our plan. When Chapman's party had come out in December they had often lost the line of flags. We believed that subsequent gales must have knocked down, destroyed or buried most of them. We had seen none during the flight on February 25th. Therefore we had to find the place by navigation. Dead reckoning would not be good enough, for the sledge wheel was inaccurate on a rough surface and it was impossible to drive the dogs straight in drifting snow.

We knew the longitude and latitude of the Station. But here was a problem. By measuring the noon altitude of the sun and making a simple calculation with the help of certain tables you can discover your latitude; but longitude is more difficult to find—for one reason because the exact Greenwich time must be known. On a long journey our half-chronometer watches would not suffice for this. We would have to take a time-signal set. But a time-signal set would add weight to our already overstrained and much repaired sledges. Besides, a few really good upsets on big snow-drifts would put it out of action. For instance, it would not have survived a journey such as Chapman's in the early winter, and we could not expect better conditions.

So we decided that we must find the Station by latitude alone—aim a few miles to the right of the Station and, when we reached the latitude, turn to the left along it until we found the place. (That was how the old sea-captains used to navigate.) Before that we would have made sure there were no flags by steering a very oblique zigzag across and across their line. To find the latitude, I had a sextant and Martin a theodolite.

As to what should happen when we reached the Station, we would relieve Courtauld of course, but the place was not to be closed down if any rations remained. Gino had said to me: "I don't think you'll have to abandon it, though of course you'll have to use your own judgment about that. We could only afford to have one man there. I don't want you to stay yourself if the journey home looks difficult. But if it looks easy to get home and the prospect of staying seems bloody —well, I'd rather you stayed yourself and sent the others back."

There is no need to describe the first part of the journey day by day. We were opposed by the combination of low temperatures and strong winds. Gordon Hayes in his *The Conquest of the North Pole* adjudged this journey from our meteorological records to be one on which "the conditions approached the limits of human endurance." I don't know about that: we could endure all right, the difficulty was to navigate and see where we were going. It warmed up in the last half, but it was very hard at first with gales and over seventy degrees of frost. I often had difficulty doing my sextant observations because the bowl of mercury for the artificial horizon started to freeze. I had to scrape the icy scum off the top. On one occasion when I did this the first thing I saw was not the reflection of the sun but of my own frozen chin. The snow surface was corrugated into steep drifts which constantly halted the dogs or upset the sledges. At our third attempt, on March 9th, we got right away and reached the Big Flag. But, travelling on, we did not find the dump at Flag 56. The loss of this food was of little importance for we had only been out a few days and still had as much as we could drag. But the fact that, after navigating as carefully as possible for less than ten miles from the Big Flag, we had, first, not seen a single one of the half-mile flags and, second, failed to distinguish the big pile which had been the dump—it showed that the blizzards had scoured the white slate clean.

In spite of this we held to our plan of steering a slight zigzag across and across the charted line—two degrees to the left and then the same to the right. For if the gales came from the middle of the Ice Cap they should not have reached the same force further in and might have left upon the surface at least a naked bamboo or an empty food tin. How excited we would have been to come upon even the droppings of a dog! But we saw nothing at all within the circular horizon except snow and the shadows which the wavelike drifts projected from the low sun. Too often we saw only flying snow, myriads of small hard hurrying grains like sand in a fast current.

My diary, written with difficulty and when tired, does not express the urgent, anxious state of mind that I remember I was in as leader of a journey which, we thought, would settle the fate of a man. But the entry for March 17th gives a hint of it.

"I dreamed last night that August turned up at the

Base before we had started. He seemed all right at first but turned out to be mad."

There was another dream which I had several times. I was going to see friends in London. I reached the street and walked to the house. But I never got further than the front-door. To open it, I would have had to take my right hand out of its glove, and I knew that my fingers would freeze to the metal handle. The fear of the pain of the skin's pulling off was too much, and it generally woke me up.

Whenever possible we made observations for latitude. But here things did not keep the rules. I quote my diary:

March 19*th, Thursday*

SCOTT — A clear day with a slight head wind. We took five hours and twenty minutes from waking to starting. (It always takes longer after lying up and the cold also helps to delay things.) We travelled for eighty minutes and then stopped for an observation. Our watches were a good bit out and it proved fortunate that we had stopped early. Martin worked the theo. with Q. booking, and I the sextant. Martin had a lot of bother getting the instrument adjusted, and the sextant iced up at once making it impossible to read. So I followed the sun up to its highest point and then packed away the instrument [to thaw it out and read it in the tent].

March 21*st, Saturday*—Still blowing and still cold and quite impossible to travel. It's annoying but let's hope it is the final gale. [The Eskimos had told us that there would be a furious final gale, so we expected each to be the last.]We are not living on the full rations and I have no luxuries left until we reach the I.C.S. The drifts are very big. Martin's sledge is completely buried except for one small piece of wood. . . .

March 22nd, Sunday—A fine day at last. We were off by nine and moving fast, but the sledges, especially mine, kept overturning which slowed us down a lot. The drifts were really bad and hardly improved throughout the day. We were going on a bearing of 27 degrees which should put us on the latitude of the I.C.S. sixteen miles to the east of it. The bearing of the drifts was 7 degrees. One of my skis which was lashed on top of my load was broken.

March 23rd, Monday—Rather a disappointing day. We had hoped to see the aeroplane and to see the flags but neither hope materialised. It was a clear morning without wind but it clouded rapidly from the sea and began to snow slightly by lunch-time. The drifts improved but in the bad light we could not see where we were going and got into trouble quite often. It felt warm camping at minus 20 degrees.

March 24th, Tuesday—Woke after a warm night to find there had only been a couple of inches of snow so had great hopes of a long day. They were in rather bad form in the other tent, having been gassed by the *cooking stove*. We took nearly six hours from waking to starting and by that time it had begun to blow. We tried to travel but the drifting snow was so thick I lost sight of the other sledges in fifty yards, so decided it was not safe. So we got the tents up again with some difficulty. It got pretty cold as soon as it started to blow but it has been amazingly warm the last twenty-four hours.

Q. the other day pushed a knife through his plate, so I gave him mine since I eat out of the pot. Martin thought he had better throw away the dud plate but threw away the good one instead.

March 25th, Wednesday—Still blowing and drifting a lot in the morning but it improved and we got off at 12.30 and went well. It was a lovely day albeit cold. We deserve a spell of fine weather, I feel.

March 26th, Thursday—Did three miles and then a latitude which I worked out roughly on the spot and it showed us six miles south of the I.C.S. latitude. So we went on six miles and camped. Since then we have worked out our results accurately and the two are pretty close, within one mile. By the chart we must be sixteen to twenty-four miles away [due east] according as we have veered east or west. I'm inclined to think that our direction was good and that our swervings account for one mile which makes us eighteen miles away.

Tonight I am back in the tent with Quintin.

RILEY — A lovely warm day. I would not swop it for an office stool for anything.

.   .   .   .   .

[The following are the diary entries which Courtauld made during this period.]

March 1st, Sunday

COURTAULD — Peter's [his brother's] 21st birthday. Wish I had something to drink his health in.

Must remember to get him a present when I get back. Had some fine sunny days lately though still a cold north-west wind. However, got the two buried ration boxes out Thank God, so now have food till end of April and could hang on till end of May. Have now been here twelve weeks alone and away from the Base over four months. Wish this good weather lasts. I am quite contented with my lot except for the bore of crawling out through the tunnel every three hours. The relieving party should have started during this last week of fine weather, in which case with decent weather and luck they should be here by the end of the month. Could certainly do with some fresh food although it is wonderful how well one keeps on these tinned rations. What would I give for a basin of green peas, new potatoes and brussel sprouts? If I were at home I might be planning a west coast cruise with W.

March 3rd, Tuesday—Still pretty fine tho' showing signs of breaking. Hope the relief party are getting on. Running very short of paraffin, so about half the day I sit or lie in darkness. Also have given up tea in the morning and drink cold water, and now have no hot supper at night. So the only hot thing I have left now is porridge in the morning and no salt for that. However, luckily one does not get hungry at this height with no exercise.

Why is it men come to these places? So many reasons have been ascribed for it. In the old days it was thought to be lust for treasure, but the treasure is gone and still men wander. Then it was craving for adventure. There is precious little adventure in sledging or in sitting on an ice cap. Is it curiosity? A yearning to look behind the veil onto the mysteries and desolations of nature in her forlorn places? Perhaps, but that is not all. Why leave all whom we love, all good friends, all creature comforts, all mindly comforts, to collect a little academic knowledge about this queer old earth of ours? What do we gain? Do we in fact morally bury ourselves in fleeing from the world? Do we simply rot or grow rank like some plant thrown over the garden wall, or do we rather come nearer to reality, see more clearly the Great Purpose behind it all in stripping our souls of the protection of our friends and in putting from us the pleasures of the body? How little the worries of the World seem to one in such a situation as this; how grand and awful that are here, the things that grip the heart with fear, the forces that spin the Universe through Space.

In leaving behind the transitory hopes and fears of pathetic humanity, does one, perhaps, come closer to the things that abide, to the forces which endure?

March 7th, Saturday—Now been here three months alone (thirteen weeks) and away from home eight months. Considering all things the time has gone by reasonably quickly though I should not mind a change of air. I reckon, unless something has gone wrong the relief should arrive between the 15th and the end of the month. One can only trust in God. If they do not arrive before the end of the month I shall be plunged in darkness and only have cold food. Weather has now broken again. Been blowing southeast gale for last twenty-four hours. Of course snow house has got filled again. Must try and dig out the tunnel at the next opportunity.

March 15th, Sunday—Been here 100 days alone. Weather has been rather good lately though still pretty cold. The sun is so bright in the middle of the day now that I have to wear dark specs. Less than two gallons of paraffin left now. Hope to Goodness the others come before it runs out or I shall have nothing to drink. Have reduced food rations and am only eating under a pound a day. However this is sufficient. It is boring sitting most of the day though. In short-lighted intervals am reading *Forsyte Saga* again. Extremely good.

March 19th, Thursday—By neglecting to stop the hole properly the night before last the snow house got completely filled up. Filled a biscuit tin and five marge tins with it but could not get out. Thought about cutting a hole in the roof of the tunnel but realised that there is about six or eight feet of snow on it outside. Eventually decided to clear the entrance to other snow house and cut a hole in the roof of that. Got into this left-hand snow house after a lot of scraping and burrowing, lying squashed down in the tunnel, but on starting to cut the hole found there was a deep drift over the top. Thought I should not be able to reach up far enough to get to the surface but eventually, after cutting through about five feet of snow, got a shaft through and with much difficulty scrambled out. How to seal it up I do not know. It is too long a shaft to close with a ration box as with the other snow house, and if I dig away the snow from the top it will make a hollow which will get drifted up and then I shall be sealed in for good.

March 22nd, Sunday— As I expected, no sooner had I got the new entrance secure against the drift than it started to blow and continued until now there is such a weight of snow on top of it that I cannot now raise the box, so I am completely buried. Paraffin has very nearly run out and things generally are pretty dismal, especially as, as far as I can tell, it is bright fine weather outside now. Just been rereading W.'s last letter. It is the only thing left to do that gives me real pleasure. However God has kept me going so far so perhaps He will see me the rest of the way. Wish I knew how everybody was at home.

March 25th, Wednesday— Been away from Base five months tomorrow. A change of diet after this time of sledging rations would certainly be acceptable. Still snowed in. [He was not able to dig himself out again.]

List of pleasures desired at Ice Cap, March 25th.

The following pleasures I should like to have granted if wishing were any good:—

1. Sitting in an arm-chair before a roaring fire listening to W. playing and singing.

2. Eight a.m. on a fine summer morning at sea at the helm of a small boat, a fresh breeze blowing, all sail set with W. and a smell of breakfast coming up to say: "Good morning."

3. Just having got into bed with clean sheets and ditto pyjamas.

4. Bright autumn morning, eating an apple in the

garden before breakfast (an enormous one):
kippers, poached eggs, kidneys and mushrooms,
cold partridge.

5. Getting into a hot bath.

.   .   .   .   .

[I return to our relief party as we turned due west along
the 67th parallel and began looking out for the Station.]

March 27th, Friday

SCOTT — A snowy morning so we did not get off
till midday. Unfortunately it cleared just too late to
get a latitude. My dogs would not keep a good course
so Q. walked in front while I drove the two teams and
Martin worked the compass. It was very warm and I
went along without windproof, hat and gloves. I had
only meant to do about seven miles but visibility was
pretty good and we seemed to see a good way on either
side so we did nine and a half miles at a good pace.
. . . We must get one [a latitude] before we leave
here, but it is snowing tonight.

March 28th, Saturday—Blew all day from the
south-east with and without snow but making an
observation and travel impossible. From a careful study
of our course I feel that we may be quite close so can
risk nothing.

Read *Henry Esmond*.

March 29th, Sunday—Weather equally bloody.

March 30th, Monday—Still the same weather. It
has been blowing from the south-east, but that has
now stopped and it's snowing again.

March 31*st, Tuesday*—A proper *gale* from the north-west.

April 1*st, Wednesday*—Not much wind but a haze which cut down visibility to a quarter of a mile. We turned out and dug out the sledges in the hope of travelling. Then we did observations. There was enough wind to shake my mercury terribly so my ob. was no good. Then it turned out that Martin's was hopeless, the readings going up and down in no sort of order. Something wrong with the theo. So we had a very cold session for nothing and could not travel with bad visibility. A poor April fool.

April 2*nd, Thursday*—A proper *gale* and cold. I fed the dogs on two lumps of pemmican and fat. Read *The Cloister and the Hearth.*

April 3*rd, Good Friday*—Did an observation before starting. Mine was a wash out but Martin got one with one vernier 67 degrees–04 minute–23 seconds. So we travelled 1·2 miles south then 8½ west but never saw a sign of the Station. It's worrying but it may be further west.

April 4*th, Saturday*—Up by four but it was snowing and blowing before we could get out of the tent. An hour later the wind veered from east to south where it stayed all day. Now it's snowing with very little wind. Visibility was of course hopeless and no chance of an observation. This is bloody.

RILEY — Things begin to look rather serious.

April 5*th, Easter* (*Sunday*)

SCOTT — Up early to a doubtful day. Completely clouded and snowing very slightly but the horizon visible all round, so we travelled. Did about four miles, when the horizon got too hazy. So we stopped and waited for a latitude. The sun was very dim behind clouds and my observation was no good. Martin only got three sights but his worked out at 67 degrees–03 minute–06 second—plumb right, though of course we can't count on it. However it adds up with the others and yet if it's right is thoroughly disturbing, for the Station can't be more than four miles further west and even that is not likely, and we don't know whether to come back parallel north or south of this line.

Today we had twenty-three lumps of pemmican left before feeding. I've given the dogs two lumps instead of three, but they can't last on that. So I decided we must start killing dogs, for if we miss the place we must keep one team fit for another journey without a rest between. Gino's will be best. Tonight I killed August, and Martin and I cut him up, but only Angus, Kumussok, Kapok, Kinilik, Pujoke and Kia-perkut ate him with much relish. I gave besides one lump of pemmican and fat. If only we get passable weather we ought to find the place. Good weather would mean a trustworthy observation, good visibility and a chance for the aeroplane. But the glass is incredibly low, 704 millibars, about 18 in. and 54 cm. by our three barometers. It's been that now for a long time. I doubt if we can stay up here more than three or four days longer, for more than that would prob-ably mean wrecking the teams, which would *muck* up another journey if that's necessary.

Q. opened his I.C.S. box—there is little hope of anything but abandoning the Station now—and gave M. and me tobacco for an Easter present. We also had an Easter tea with marmalade.

RILEY — I read through the Communion service after breakfast. I wish I was able to make Communion. I do miss it. . . . We can look for the Station for three more days only and then we shall have to return to the Base. I pray God we find August first for it will go hard with him if we don't. He may walk out, but he will have to cut up the tent. . . . Of course he may have done this and that is why we have not spotted the Station.

.   .   .   .   .

[After his entry on March 25th, Courtauld next wrote his diary on this same day. He had remained entombed since March 21st and had a minimum of fuel for either heat or light. This is his entry for Easter Day.]

April 5th, Sunday

COURTAULD — Now been here alone four months. No sign of relief. Only about a cupful of paraffin left and one or two candles. Have to lie in darkness almost all the time. Chocolate finished and tobacco almost (half a pouch left). What a change from last Easter at Falmouth or the one before at Abbotsbury. What wouldn't I give to be living either the one or the other again or to be with you my dearest. But if it were not for having you to think about as I lie in the dark and cannot sleep

144

life would be intolerable. I wonder what you are doing. If I could be sure you were happy I wouldn't mind. But I trust in God absolutely. I am sure He does not mean me to die alone here and never see you again. If I didn't I could not be singing your songs or keeping cheerful as I am. Oh, that fatal day 9 months ago [when the *Quest* sailed from London]. Why did I ever leave you?

.　　.　　.　　.　　.

April 6th, Monday

SCOTT — Woke early to hear snow on the tent. But it improved later and we got off by 9.15. It cleared beautifully for a warm latitude. Martin and I got within 5 seconds of each other. Mine worked out at 67 degrees–02 minute–10 seconds which adds up with the last trustworthy observation we got just before reaching the latitude. So we went on the same course for a bit over 2 miles. Then having travelled 26½ miles along the latitude and being able to see 2½ to 3 miles further we decided we must have passed the place, and so went 2 miles due north and then started back [eastwards] from there parallel to the old course. But how we have passed the Station I don't know unless it is thoroughly drifted over.

It was very pleasant walking but it got colder when we camped. I picked up a dead snow bunting which must have died last night. The dogs were in very good form. If only the aeroplane would come up now we ought to find the place, if it is to be found, but even without the aeroplane we must surely see it if we have time to travel back like this two miles north of our old course and then again two miles south of it.

April 7th, Tuesday

RILEY — We carried on one mile N. of the Lat. of the Station. This was confirmed by a midday observation. We covered 12·7 miles in all. We must have passed it and we are now east of it. Tomorrow we shall go one mile south which will put us on the latitude and travel 13 to 14 miles along it. If we don't run over the Station I fear something has happened to August and he is dead for we must have passed within a mile south and north of the Station which we know was visible from that distance. It would appear therefore that he has been dead some time for it to drift over as completely as it must have. However tomorrow we may find it. If we don't there is no more we can do without a time-signal set.

SCOTT — We have a minimum of dog food. In the evening it clouded and blew from the north. Pray God we are not in for another spell of bad weather.

April 8th, Wednesday—A day without visibility. First snowing and then blowing from the north about 25 m.p.h.

April 9th, Thursday— Still hopeless visibility. We can't do more now than travel between our other two legs along the latitude and pray God we find the place. Read *The Cloister and the Hearth*, a good book by a cynic with a sense of humour, and it keeps my mind off the bloodiness of all this.

RILEY — I had a touch of snow blindness last night.

146

THE FIRST RELIEF ATTEMPT

SCOTT — We have been beaten. Up early and off by 8.45, a fine day with very good visibility. We travelled obliquely for two miles. I saw one of our old flags three-quarters of a mile away and walked down to it to make sure. [We had put in a few flags as a check while beating up and down.]

Then we travelled for twelve miles along the latitude between our other two legs. Every 300 yards or so I stood on the sledge and looked round, but never a sign of the Station. For the last few miles the topography was obviously wrong—quite flat all round. So we turned for home and did 2·6 miles before camping.

We will have to hurry for home now. We have only four days' dog food at full ration for the dogs. At two-third rations it will last six days and we have not too much man food. I can't make out why we have not seen the Station unless August is parangilak [destroyed and finished] and the place is completely drifted up, or unless we have made a complete *mess* of the longitude which I can't understand. Anyway I don't think we could do anything useful by staying longer for it would inevitably mean losing most of the dogs, and if we can get back quickly now there may be another chance.

RILEY — Poor August's people and Molly [the lady Courtauld referred to as W.]. Unless he has walked out they will have six weeks of suspense at least.

.   .   .   .   .

147

"If we can get back quickly now there may be another chance."

For the first few miles after I had taken the decision to turn back we looked over our shoulders right and left continually. But after that the only hope was in hurrying. We were not capable of much speed. But visibility did not matter now—we travelled on a compass bearing through any weather— and we did not sleep for more than four hours at night. On the seventh day we hit off the Big Flag almost exactly.

That was satisfactory but not entirely so. It meant that we had wasted no travelling distance, but it suggested that we had started out from where we thought we had. Since we had found the Big Flag starting from the position of the Ice Cap Station, why had we failed to find the Ice Cap Station when starting from the Big Flag?

At the Big Flag we found rations and gear which had been dumped by Stephenson's party. Stephenson, Chapman and Bingham had been due to set off for Mount Forel and Kangerdlugssuaq after we had left the Base. They must have come back early. Presumably the weather had been too bad for them. But the important thing was that as a result there must be more dogs at the Base. That at least was a good thing.

We hurried on, driving straight over the crevasses now safely bridged by drifted snow. We reached the top of Bugbear Bank at sunset. We halted, as we always used to do, at the spot where the Base first came in sight. The dogs lay down immediately, flat on their sides with their tongues lolling out. We sat on the sledges and looked down the slopes of the glacier which at first were as steep as the instep of a foot, then flattened out as the toes reached down among the first bare rocks to the edge of the frozen sea. Beyond was the fjord, grey with the rotting snow of spring; and then the promontory on which was the Base hut, indistinguishable at that distance in the dusk.

We had pressed on to camp here during the darkest hours, but having got so far we found it was impossible to stop. We woke the dogs and slithered down Bugbear Bank. There the sledges stuck in the soft deep snow. So we left them, loosed the dogs and walked on through the darkness.

I suppose the temperature was about freezing point, but to us whose standard was fifty or sixty degrees colder it seemed enervatingly hot. Our snow shoes sank deep into the snow which spilled into the hole on top of them so that we had to lift that weight at every step. I expect it was largely mental exhaustion but in any case I felt utterly done. The Base used to be a magnet which drew one more and more strongly in spite of weariness. But now it repelled: I did not want to arrive. I thought of them waking up and crowding out of their bunks with questions. Why had we come back without August? I believed there had been a good reason but could not remember what it was. I was as low in spirit and body as I hope ever to be, plodding through muddy snow unwillingly towards the sleeping hut.

When the dogs started their howling, meeting the

others, Chapman came out of the hut, then Gino in
pyjamas.

Gino listened to our story with perfect calmness,
and directly afterwards settled down to work out
stores and equipment for the next journey and to
prepare a message for England. He told me that I had
been right in turning back when I had, for conse-
quently there was time for another relief journey.
Courtauld must still have food, he said, and the
weather should by now be fit for taking in a time-
signal set and finding the Station by exact navigation.

But I don't think that Quintin, Martin and I were
hopeful as we climbed dizzy with tiredness into our
bunks. Gino would find the Station. But would he find
Courtauld alive and sane? When I shut my eyes I
saw the Ice Cap as it had been while we were hunting
up and down. The shadows of the snow drifts had
been as confusing as camouflage. But we must have
passed close to the Station. We would have seen it if
it were still above the surface. Therefore the tent
with August Courtauld in it must be buried. And
people who are buried are generally dead.

CHAPTER XI

Climax

THE last phase might equally be described from four different points of view—Courtauld's, that of the second relief journey, that of those waiting at the Base and that of the people in England and the rest of the outside world. Our concern is principally with the first two, and a little with the third; but the last cannot be ignored for it was still the Ice Cap, the mysterious Ice Cap, which was the cause of so much anxiety and consequent action. So I shall try to combine the four aspects of the story.

While Lindsay, Riley and I were hurrying to the Base, Courtauld had written in his diary on April 13th: "Finished my last pipe of baccy today. There is now precious little left to live for. Can have light only for meals which consist of porridge just warmed up, biscuit, cold pemmican and marge. This means that the house has got very cold and is covered with hoar-frost up to the roof. Still impossible to get outside. Feet keep on freezing up and have to be always taking off socks and warming them with my hands. Hardly any paraffin left, or candles. I suppose I shall soon be reduced to chewing snow. At present am reduced to a pint of water a day and under a pound of food. I wonder if *Cariad* is cruising now. What wouldn't I give to be aboard her and eating beef and onion pudding. I would give an eye to be home now with you my own and see you yourself instead of only your poor old pipe for which I have no tobacco."

Lindsay, Riley and I reached the Base, as I have said, at midnight April 17th-18th. By three o'clock that same morning Gino was ready to start on another relief journey with Chapman and Rymill. (He had been prepared, I think, for such an eventuality since Stephenson's party had been driven back so early in their attempt to reach the Mount Forel district.) He also drafted a message to the Committee in London which Lemon was to tap out at his next wireless schedule. In this he said that my party had returned without finding the Station but that owing to the severe conditions we might have passed within a quarter of a mile without seeing it. He added that Courtauld must still have food and that he, Watkins, was about to lead another relief. But he concluded: "There is always the possibility that Courtauld is not alive, or unwell, in which case the Station is probably completely covered."

This, as may well be imagined, set things moving in England.

As it happened, bad weather prevented Watkins from starting for three days. While his party waited at the Base, the dogs which were to draw their sledges prowled and scavenged in the thawing snow about the hut. At sea-level, winter was already dead and rotting.

Meanwhile, on April 20th, Courtauld lit his candle for a few minutes and recorded: "Only one candle left.

152

Hardly any paraffin. Lie in the dark all day designing the ideal cruise and the ideal meal. Left foot swelling up. Hope it isn't scurvy."

Next morning, April 21st, the relief party set out. Stephenson, Wager, Bingham and I started with them to give assistance on the first steep slopes. Parting, we saw the three sledges drive away in single file over the white horizon. After that we could only go back to the Base and wait for their return—in three or six or even eight weeks' time.

I don't think that any of us doubted they would find the place. Winter had given place to summer on the Ice Cap. The snow surface was smooth and the temperature comparatively mild. As a result the party had been able to take a time-signal set and could fix their position to within a hundred yards square. They were all competent navigators, Rymill particularly. It was he who had originally worked out the position of the Ice Cap Station when we had set it up the last summer. He, with Gino and Freddie, would certainly find the tent even if they had to prod the snow over the calculated spot. . . . But what would they find inside it? None of us at the Base was prepared completely to commit himself. It was a period of tension and suspense.

On April 22nd, the day after Gino's party had vanished over the white horizon, we received by wireless the first reaction to his message to England. The Committee expressed great anxiety about Courtauld and asked a number of questions. Lemon answered them, said that Watkins did not consider the position desperate and that everything possible was being done. To be frank, we were a little touchy.

That was all that we in Greenland then knew of what was happening in England. But on April 23rd the Committee felt that they must release such information as they possessed and sent a brief statement to *The Times*, which had our press rights. *The Times* published it next day under the heading: "Anxiety for the Safety of Mr. Courtauld."

It was not likely to stop there. Other papers took it up. Here was a member of a great family which everybody knew or knew of, "Marooned on an Ice Cap." During the following days some remarkable stories were published. One was headed: "Danger from Wolves." The best—if anyone had been in the mood to appreciate it—appeared in a French paper. This stated that Mlle Augustine Courtauld, the only female member of the Expedition, had spent the winter alone 140 miles from the rest of the party and that every attempt by the men to reach her had been unsuccessful.

For the first time in its millions of years of existence the Ice Cap had come into the news—however inaccurately.

Meanwhile, travelling over the Ice Cap at about ten miles each day, Watkins, Rymill and Chapman were carefully navigating towards the Station. Their chief hardship was sunburn which cracked their lips and made their peeling faces most painfully sensitive to the cold winds which still occasionally blew.

Meanwhile also, the object of their search wrote in

his diary on April 26th: "Just six months since we left the Base and started on sledge rations. Been here alone twenty weeks. Everything running out. Using last candle. V. little paraffin. What I shall do for drinking water I don't know. Only two more biscuits. In four days I officially run out of food but have a reserve, Thank God, of pemmican and marge. Smoking tea as I have no fuel to cook it with."

Next day we at the Base received a message from the Committee saying that a large Swedish aeroplane chartered by them and piloted by Captain Ahrenberg was about to fly out to us from Malmo via Iceland to help in locating the Station and dropping supplies to the sledge party. There were also plans for sending an ice-breaker with fuel and other supplies.

This was a glimpse of the activity which our brief message had caused at home. More important, we realised that the news about Courtauld must be public property. We had only communicated with the Committee and in our innocent isolation believed that the Press and public knew nothing. But if a relief flight were being planned the secret must be out. Lacking news there would be rumours. Also, defensively, we were afraid that outsiders might come to our 'rescue.' So we prepared and sent a long message to *The Times*. This gave a full account of what had led up to the present situation. We tried to make it plain that we were doing all that could usefully be done.

This was published on April 30th. But the Ice Cap was front-page news by now in most British newspapers and many abroad. One stated: "A wireless message was received today from Mr. Augustine Courtauld . . . who is marooned on an Ice Cap in Greenland, which runs: 'Absolutely without provisions.'" Absurd and immoral though this statement was, it happened to be very near the truth.

Courtauld's diary entry for May 1st was: "No sign of relief. Shall have to think of walking soon if I can get out. Biscuits finished also candles. Am burning ski-wax for a light but it makes nasty smoke. Have no sugar as the last tin is outside. Food has officially run out but I still have a fair amount of essentials, though lemon juice [the only anti-scorbutic] is running low which is pretty serious."

Captain Ahrenberg's monoplane had been delayed by bad weather. Meanwhile Hampton at Angmagssalik, thirty miles from the Base, was working desperately hard to get one of our two little Moths into the air. Both had been badly damaged by ice or storms. Hampton was using driftwood and shirt material to make up for his lack of spare parts.

But Ahrenberg's was not the only aeroplane which was planning to come to us. We had already heard several times by radio from Professor Alexander Johanssen—he always signed himself in full—who was sailing in an Iceland patrol ship to the edge of the pack-ice, intending to fly from there. His messages were questionnaires. (Later we discovered that he had a reporter on board.) And there was more than one other rescue attempt, which we did not know about, being privately planned. The English Press mentioned as a possibility "R.A.F. Aid."

But all these gallant volunteers were checked by one fundamental difficulty—the almost ingenious isolation of the Ice Cap at this season. Any machine flying out would have to take off on wheels or floats. The only landing areas in Greenland were the fjords —and these were still frozen. Skis would be necessary for anything except a crash landing. Outside the frozen fjords was the jumbled mass of heavy pack-ice drifting down from the polar basin. Not even an ice-breaker could get through for weeks to come.

This is my diary record of May 2nd at the Base: "Ham arrived just as we were finishing breakfast with a much-patched aeroplane and the news [from the Danish radio operator at Angmagssalik] that Professor Alex took off in the grey dawn [from the outer edge of the pack-ice] but came down again immediately owing to engine failure, and has gone back to Reykjavik. We wonder. Then we heard that Ahrenberg had left [Reykjavik] at 11.40 and wanted us to make 'much smoke.' So Ham and D'Aeth and I went down to the ice with a bath and oil and petrol and kept a beautiful fire going till 7 p.m. when we heard that he had turned back owing to fog.

"In the morning D'Aeth and Q. flew in [over the Ice Cap] with dog food. [It was Quintin's first flight in an aeroplane.] But they were turned back after seventy miles—again by fog."

After Hampton's tremendous efforts it was bad luck that D'Aeth and Riley in the Moth had not seen the sledge party. But this must mean that Watkins, Chapman and Rymill were more than seventy miles inland. On the whole we were excited and pleased.

Naturally we had sent home no message about Watkins' party since they had started their journey on April 21st. There was nothing more to say about it. For three weeks at least no news, if it were not necessarily good news, could certainly not be bad. But a few newspapers used a different interpretation of this silence. A London evening paper stated: "There are now four Englishmen lost in the icy wastes of Greenland."

During the first days of May the number of prospective rescue attempts increased in number. "Seven Expeditions for Arctic Rescue" was a headline on May 4th. Only two of these had actually left their homes—Professor Alexander Johanssen, who had come as far as the edge of the pack-ice and turned back, and Captain Ahrenberg, who was waiting in Iceland for good weather, bravely prepared to accept the risk of crashing on the Greenland ice.

There were, of course, no reporters in Greenland, nor within hundreds of miles. But on May 5th there was published an article which was dated "Angmagssalik, Greenland, Monday," and read: "There is hardly any curtain more difficult to penetrate than that which the lonely Arctic wastes can drop behind those that are cut off from the outposts of civilisation. Bad luck has dogged the efforts of those who are searching for Mr. Courtauld, and this task is rendered more difficult and anxious by the disappearance of Mr. Watkins, Mr. Rymill and Mr. Chapman of the

British Arctic Air Route Expedition who set out fourteen days ago in sledges to find Mr. Courtauld.

"As they had only enough provisions to last for a few weeks, apprehension for their safety increases with every hour which passes without receiving word from them. They are believed to be roaming somewhere on the vast ice sheet in the interior of the country.

"Rescue operations are being pressed forward with feverish activity. . . ."

As it happened, May 5th was the day of climax—a quiet climax as befitted the Ice Cap, which for all its faults is essentially dignified. On the evening of May 3rd, Watkins, Rymill and Chapman had camped, they believed, within a couple of miles of the Station. The next morning broke stormy, with drifting snow. They decided to remain where they were until they were able to fix their position exactly.

In the evening the weather cleared. It was by then too late in the day to make an observation, but leaving the tent standing they skied off in different directions to hunt. Watkins and Chapman returned at about ten o'clock, Rymill at midnight. They had quartered the possible area but none of them had seen any sign of the Station.

May 5th was beautifully fine. They set up the time-signal aerial and the theodolite and took observations for longitude and latitude. Careful and unhurried, Rymill worked these out. They were one mile northwest of the Station.

The three men put on their skis and each took a dog on a lead. They spread out into an extended line which covered about half a mile. Then they advanced towards the spot.

The Ice Cap, as the reader knows, seems level but in fact is undulated into wide and very gentle dunes. Since everything is white and similar you may think that you can see all that there is around you when actually there is dead ground in each depression. The three men were moving at right angles to these dunes. They topped one—and simultaneously saw a small dark object in front.

They raced towards this. Very soon they recognised it as the tattered remains of the half-buried Union Jack. The tops of one or two meteorological instruments were also showing. But the courtyard wall, the two snow houses, the dome-shaped tent itself had completely disappeared. The Ice Cap had done what it impartially would do to any artificial excrescence— buried it. Without ceaseless opposition it must have buried it, wiped the canvas clean, four or five months ago. . . .

They were climbing the slope of the tumulus before they noticed that the brass ventilating pipe was just projecting above the surface.

Watkins knelt down above it, called August's name, and waited a long second for a reply.

.   .   .   .   .

COURTAULD — *May* 6th (*Wednesday*). Written on sledge returning to the Base.

Yesterday was the greatest day in my life. All Monday I kept on wondering what it was that May

The Ice Cap Station : In Autumn

As found in Spring

Courtald on his return to the Base

Gino Watkins

5th should be famous for. I could not think of anybody's birthday or any event so I decided it must be
that the relief was going to arrive. Yesterday (May
5th) the primus gave its last gasp as I was melting
water for the morning meal. I was lying in my bag
after this so-called meal of a bit of pemmican and
margarine and had just decided that I should have to
start and walk back on June 1st if I could get out,
when suddenly there was an appalling noise like a bus
going by followed by a confused yelling noise. I nearly
jumped out of my skin. Was it the house falling in at
last? A second later I realised the truth. It was somebody, some real human voice, calling down the ventilator. It was a wonderful moment. I could not think
what to do or say. I yelled back some stuttering remarks
that seemed quite futile for the occasion. "Hooray,"
they shouted. "Are you all right?" "Yes, thank God
you've come. I am perfectly fit." "Thank God," they
said. It was Gino and Freddie; they were as relieved
as I was. The whole world seemed turned inside out.
At one moment I was lying in the dark wondering
how ever I was going to see anybody again or ever get
home, and the next home was in sight. It was bright
sunshine they said outside and they had reached by
navigation a place about two miles away where they
had camped and from which they had gone out on skis
to find the Station. They told of many happenings.
Apparently Jamie, Martin and Quintin had been up
in March but had failed to find the Station, so directly
they got back Gino, Freddie and John Rymill started
off equipped with the best navigation gear and had

reached me in fifteen days from the Base. They said the going was excellent and that I should be able to ride the whole way back. This was an incredible relief to hear, for with my weakened condition I could never have walked or skied it. Very soon Gino had smashed a hole in the roof and let in the blinding sunshine and blue sky, blinding even with dark snow glasses on. The next moment they had dropped through the hole and we were grasping hands and thanking God that the job was done. They told of the many flights to find me in the winter and the smashing of the machines, of the difficulties of sledging on the coast owing to open water, of the frightful gales worse this year than any before making travel in the winter impossible, of Wager nearly losing his life down a crevasse, of D'Aeth getting his arm smashed by the aeroplane propeller, of B. and R. getting married and of their having gone to America, of the friendliness of the Eskimos. . . .

They pulled me out through the roof and I found myself pretty weak after nearly two months snowed up. However I managed to ski slowly about half-way to the camp when John met me with his sledge and I could ride. It was all too good to be true. To get into a dry warm tent with a roaring primus and plenty of food and light again. I found I could eat only very little and did not try to take much. I was and still am unbelievably happy. That my trust in God's goodness should have been so wonderfully justified and that now I could sledge comfortably back in the warm early summer and get back to good friends whom I might never have seen again, and then later in the summer to sail south to see W. again and all the family.

I could not sleep at all last night from excitement, and so after a real hot meal of porridge we packed up and sledged to the Station to collect the valuables. It was heartrending to see the quantities of food which we threw away since they had brought five weeks' food and we expect to get back in eight or ten days.

To see them make a bonfire with a tin of paraffin— a tin I would have given a fortune for a day ago. It is a wonderful bright cloudless day with hot sun. I have a comfortable place on sleeping-bags on one sledge and am writing as we go smoothly along. One man walks in front to lead the way and the last sledge takes compass bearings on him to check the course. All the flags are buried so that the compass is the only guide. It is very like sailing across a dead white sea. A level horizon circles us in and there is nothing to look at but the dazzling white snow and the intense blue sky. We have collected as much of the stuff from the Ice Cap Station as we could be bothered with. Of course a lot has been left behind—books, clothes, etc. But that cannot be helped as we want to travel as fast as possible, and we have a lot of extra dog food which we cannot afford to throw away.

Although the winter work has been pretty well washed out by the weather and the flight to Canada stopped by the bursting of the Moths, yet the inde-fatigable Gino has plenty of plans up his sleeve. At present Steve and Wager accompanied by the Doc are trying to climb Mt. Forel. Then when we get back Jamie and a party are going to sledge to Julianahaab. Then John and Freddie are going across to Holstein-borg, and finally Gino, Lemon and someone are going south round Cape Farewell to Julianahaab mapping the coast. I have had enough of sledging ice caps and boat journeys.

It is more wonderful than words can express to be free out of that dark place under the snow and to be really going home. . . .

.   .   .   .   .

Huskies do not bark. They make excited, angry, challenging noises like other dogs, and then for deeper expression change into a howl—high-pitched, wild, wavering, a sort of canine yodel or, for the imaginative, a libretto to the unheard music of the Northern Lights. It is so infectious that every dog within a mile must join in, so intense and long sustained that your eardrums are near bursting and your nerves at twanging point.

To this chorus Watkins, Chapman, Rymill and Courtauld walked into the Base hut at four o'clock in the morning on Tuesday, May 12th. Gino was neatly brushed and shaved as ever; Courtauld's hair was on his shoulders and his beard on his chest—like some hermit prophet from the Old Testament.

We had been out of our bunks at the first sound, with Ahrenberg and the two men of his crew who were sleeping with us. Ahrenberg, after a daring and successful arrival, had flown in four days before with D'Aeth and seen the party ski-ing out beside their sledges—so we had known what to expect. But that did not reduce the warmth and excitement of our greeting.

Later, when Courtauld had washed and shaved and sent a message home, he and I went out to get some ptarmigan for the pot. We scrambled about on the black mountains which kept the Ice Cap back.

CHAPTER XII

Finishing Touches

ON the same day that Courtauld returned to the Base, Professor Wegener's body was found by Dr. Weiken, Dr. Sorge and five Eskimos. Against the common background—one cannot describe the impersonal Ice Cap as an enemy—we had been lucky and they had not.

Dr. Kurt Wegener came out to take his brother's place. The Germans got all the necessary instruments and supplies up to Eismitte and completed their programme very well, doing echo soundings of the ice depth and a lot more besides in their thorough, absorbedly scientific way.

We, in our somewhat different way, finished our expedition in fine style. In July Stephenson, Lindsay and I galloped and skied across the Ice Cap, southwestward to Ivigtut on the other coast, 450 miles in four weeks. We enjoyed a dream of a summer sledge journey, sleeping in the warmth of day, travelling in the gentle frost of night with Viking sails on the sledges, the sun only dipping below the horizon for an hour or two so that the sunset clouds had no time to lose their colours before they were rekindled to announce the dawn. This journey, after what had gone before, seemed smooth and exciting as a flight above the clouds.

FINISHING TOUCHES

At the beginning of August, Rymill and Hampton began a direct east to west crossing to Holsteinborg. At this warmest season they met the dangers and difficulties of opening crevasses, slush and rivers. But they took kayaks with them on their sledges and reached the west coast settlements calmly and in their own time.

Meanwhile Watkins, Lemon and Courtauld were making a 600-mile open-boat journey down the east coast and round the southern point of Greenland, often in danger from the excretions of the Ice Cap, the dropping of icebergs from the glacier-ends.

Thus by several routes we made our way southward, over or round the Ice Cap. Half of us first met again in Copenhagen. There, at a reception, dazzled, deafened and overwhelmed by the hospitality of the Danish hosts, two smallish close-cropped men came up to me. The first clicked his heels, bowed and said, "Georgi." The second clicked his heels, bowed and said, "Sorge." And immediately we were in conversation once more upon the Ice Cap. Different in nationality, upbringing and humour—and soon to be enemies—we were united by a common experience.

Between then and the war there were several expeditions to Greenland. Lindsay, who led the British Trans-Greenland Expedition of 1934, made a most remarkable 1,000-mile journey on the Ice Cap. And Courtauld and Wager, with their wives, returned to climb the mountains, the highest in the Arctic, which Watkins had discovered from the air.

The Ice Cap came into the war. Greenland was

found to be doubly important, as a link on the land-bridged Great Circle route between North America and Europe—the Arctic Air Route was used for transporting combat planes—and for reports on one of the main sources of Europe's weather.

A number of aeroplanes came down on the Ice Cap for one reason or another. A Flying Fortress crashed near the southern end of it in November 1942. One broken arm was the only serious casualty. When the crew had repaired their radio they discovered that they were close to the coast, only twenty-five miles from a weather-and-rescue station. Within a fortnight they began to be supplied by air drops. But they were experts of a highly mechanical trade, only by chance and much against their will upon the Ice Cap. They were surrounded by crevasses and the weather was fierce. So they waited, with admirable fortitude, until at last they were rescued by air. But this took five months, in the course of which five men lost their lives while another contracted gangrened feet as a result of frost-bite.

In July of the next year two bombers and four fighters were flying to Europe by the Greenland route. Having crossed the east coast they were turned back by bad weather, and they asked in code for instructions where to land, for more than one auxiliary field was available. The reply came back in the same code ordering them northwards. The weather grew worse, but the order to head north was repeated. At last all six machines ran out of fuel and came down on the Ice Cap.

FINISHING TOUCHES

Those six aeroplanes are still on the Ice Cap. The mystery of the order to fly north was never explained. It was sent by no Allied station. It can only have come either from a U-boat or from one of the German weather stations which were concealed here and there on Greenland's east coast.

Operation Holzauge consisted of the setting up of one such station and its maintenance from the summer of 1942 to 1943. The *Sachsen*, a diesel-driven trawler, slipped unnoticed across the North Atlantic and established a base on Sabine Island. The commander was Lieutenant Ritter, who had been a Spitsbergen trapper before the war.

Meteorological observations were made and several times daily transmitted by radio to Tromso. All went well for five months. The ship and hut were well concealed from the air, and the whole rough, thousand-mile long, deeply indented coast was practically uninhabited.

There was, however, the Greenland Sledge Patrol. This had been formed in 1941. It consisted of Danish and Norwegian hunters and some Eskimos. These men were in fact hired by the U.S. Army and their duty was to patrol the east coast as far north as latitude 77 degrees, visiting the few and scattered hunting cabins and keeping a look-out for signs of enemy landings.

On March 13th a unit of the Sledge Patrol consisting of a Dane, Marius Jensen, and two Eskimos came on a German hunting party on the coast near Sabine Island.

They were also seen by the Germans. They had put their heads into a hornets' nest. They ran for their base at Eskimonaes, nearly a hundred miles away. Lt. Ritter, who had no less than sixteen men under his command, sent a powerful force to catch them before they could tell of their discovery. Jensen and the two Eskimos just managed to escape on skis, but they lost their sledges, their dog teams and their log book.

Returning with this booty, the Germans reported the incident by wireless to Tromso.

They received a reply from the Oberkommando der Kriegsmarine. They were to attack and destroy the patrol base and radio at Eskimonaes.

Ritter with five well-armed men set out, using the captured dog sledges. With rifles, automatics and hand grenades—all the disconcerting din of a blitzkrieg attack—they advanced upon the huts. The inmates, who had nothing except hunting rifles and hunting ammunition and were entirely unused to such behaviour, got out quickly. But they took a portable transmitter with them, and used it.

Lt. Ritter left this message:

"March 24th: The U.S.A. protects its defence interests here in Greenland. We do the same also. We are not at war with Denmark. But the administration on Greenland gave orders to capture or shoot us, and besides that you gave weather reports to the enemy. You are making Greenland into a place of war. We have stayed quietly at our posts without attacking you. Now you want war, so you shall have war. But remember that if you shoot with illegal weapons [soft-nosed hunting bullets] which you have at hand here in the loft of the radio station, then you must take full responsibility for the consequences, because you are placing yourselves outside the rules of war. Note we have put all personal effects of the hunters and all pelts in this hut, while we have destroyed the radio apparatus operating for the U.S.A. (Signed) Commandant of the German Wehrmacht Detail in Eskimonaes."

On his way back to Sabine Island, Ritter and his party met Marius Jensen and two fellow Danes who were returning from a patrol northwards. Jensen and Nilsen were captured. The third man, Knudsen, tried to escape and was shot and killed. It is worth noticing that this is the first man-against-man casualty which has been recorded. Knudsen was buried under a Danish flag and a pile of stones.

Lt. Ritter took his two captives as far as Germania Harbour, close to his ship. There he decided to release Nilsen. He sent a patrol of four Germans with two sledges to scatter the station at Ella Island, beyond Eskimonaes, about three hundred miles to the south. Ritter himself, taking his prisoner Jensen as guide, set out on a reconnaissance in the neighbourhood of Myggbukta.

The patrol of four returned to their Base on Sabine Island, not having found anyone at Ella. They were surprised that Ritter was not back before them, for he had had a shorter distance to travel.

A few days later, the Americans attacked the

Sabine Island Base with Liberators and Flying Fortresses. The installations were bombed and straffed for two hours. The Germans, who had had time to scatter, suffered no casualties. But that was the end of Operation Holtzauge. With their equipment destroyed they could do no more, and were evacuated by air.

But the fate of Lt. Ritter, the leader of the party, is still to be described. As soon as he and his prisoner Jensen reached Myggbukta, Jensen overpowered him. Then there began a fantastic 350-mile journey, the two men, their *rôles* reversed, still inevitably eating and sleeping together. After four weeks Jensen handed over his former captor as a prisoner to the Station at Scoresby Sound.

In 1944 a certain Franz Nusser suggested that it would be much safer to set up a weather station actually on the Ice Cap, digging it into the ice for concealment. It was to be supplied from the air. Dr. Georgi modified this plan, suggesting that the Station should be near the middle line of the Ice Cap. The plan was never put into operation because by then Germany had nothing to spare for such ventures.

But, for peace-time science, this technique was used, and it proved excellent for defence against the rigours of the Ice Cap itself.

In 1949 the Frenchman Paul-Emile Victor established a weather station as near as possible to the site of Eismitte. It was done in a grand manner which would have been impossible twenty years earlier even if the money had been available. From the west coast a convoy of twenty-two men with five Weasels (light tracked vehicles), two trailer laboratories and seven sledges carrying 17,600 lb. of stores travelled onto the Ice Cap. When they were about half-way their four-engined Liberator flew from Iceland and dropped them spare parts for the Weasels and six tons of food and fuel. Two days later, July 17th, the convoy reached the site of La Station Centrale.

They burrowed into the ice, digging out living quarters, store rooms and laboratories connected by a system of tunnels over 300 yards long. Their Liberator made thirteen flights from Iceland during the second half of July and bombed them with fifteen tons of food and twenty-five tons of fuel. Thus eight men were enabled to pass the winter comfortably and studiously while the storms raged above, finding no obstruction to tear down or cover in drift.

On the Ice Cap, the best protection against being buried is to bury yourself. Nothing may mark for long the huge white canvas which we set out to paint.

Printed in Great Britain
at Hopetoun Street, Edinburgh,
by T. and A. CONSTABLE LTD.
Printers to the University of Edinburgh